About the Authors ...

Randy McLelland

I met Robbie Farmer during the summer of 1969, when her family moved to the town of Mont Belvieu, Texas, thirteen miles north of Baytown. We met the Sunday she and her family joined the church where I was a member. I was about to be a freshman in high school; she would be entering junior high.

Robbie and I both loved music. Piano was her specialty and I was a guitar player. Over the next five years, we began to blend our music together at church. During our high school years, Robbie became the church pianist and I became involved in leading the music. We also started to sing together and began to receive invitations to perform at events.

Halfway through her senior year, I asked Rob to go out on a real date. She accepted. We went to Pizza Hut! From that night, our relationship changed and deepened. Then on July 16, 1977, we were married. She was about to start her junior year in college and I was a pipefitter for Brown and Root. We moved to Pasadena, Texas, not far from where I had lived during my early childhood.

Robbie and I joined the church where I was saved when I was eight years old. We were very active there, involved with the music program, as well as working with the youth and college students. After about three years, our pastor, Brother Pete Bradfield, asked me if I would consider leaving my job and coming on staff as the youth minister. I declined.

But Brother Pete was persistent. He talked with me a few more times about the youth ministry position. My typical answer became, "Brother Pete, God's not calling me to full-time ministry!" One day I gave that response and he came back with, "Son, (I *hated* it when he did that!) HE'S calling. YOU'RE not listening!" More frustration came from knowing he was right.

After a time of struggling with God's obvious call on my life, I made the decision to go into full-time youth ministry at twenty-nine years old. The church in Pasadena had, by then, called someone else to that position. We now had our first child, Rachael, who was not quite two at the time. Our first church job as youth minister was part-time in Calvert, Texas at the church my parents attended. We were there for about a year and a half. Our son, Reid, was born during this time. In the summer of 1986, we were offered the position of being full-time youth minister in the small, north central, cotton-growing community of Haskell, Texas. We moved there that August.

Three years and one month later, on her thirty-second birthday, Robbie woke up with significant and unexplained pain in the joints of her hands. We would learn over the next several weeks that she was battling Lupus, an autoimmune disease. This would be an on-going struggle, since Lupus was, and is, incurable.

In the fall of 1997, we were given the incredible opportunity to pursue a long-time dream of having our own ministry. It would involve preaching, concerts, and providing clean entertainment for various events. In December that year, we moved to Glen Rose, Texas, an hour south of Fort Worth. Six years later would find us not only establishing *Livin' It Up Ministries*, but also following God's lead to start a new church. *Cornerstone Christian Fellowship* was born on January 19, 2003.

Robbie, although struggling more and more with Lupus, was very active in our church. She played keyboard, guitar, and mandolin in our praise and worship band and started leading a ladies' Bible study. On Sunday, December 19, 2010, Robbie suffered an aneurism of her aorta. Twelve hours later, shortly after midnight, at the Texas Heart Institute in Houston, Robbie finally won the battle with Lupus as she stepped into Heaven with her Lord, Whom she loved and served faithfully for some forty-six years.

Shortly after moving to Haskell, I had met Kevin Walker. I was on staff at First Baptist Church and Kevin was serving at Eastside Baptist Church, on the other side of town. (Remember—it's a SMALL town!) Kevin and his wife, Julie, also worked with the student ministries in their church.

Kevin was a tremendous worship leader and was simply great on the keyboard. We worked together at many youth camps in our area. Julie was often at the camps with us, but was usually working as a sponsor for the girls from their church, so our paths rarely crossed.

Kevin and Julie had their first child, Adrienne, in 1988 shortly before leaving Haskell in 1989, after serving at Eastside for six and a half years. They joined a former pastor/friend at a church in Lampasas to continue their ministry and were there for four years. During this time, their son, Jared, was born.

I would hear from Kevin occasionally and knew he and the family had made another move to a large church in Arlington, Texas. Kevin became the Worship Pastor at Pantego Bible Church. In 1999, he invited me to come be a part of a special worship service at Pantego. It was the first time I'd seen him in ten years. A few years later, I learned that the Walkers had moved to Colorado to start a new ministry and we lost touch from that point on.

In 2009, mutual friends informed me that Kevin was battling Lymphoma. I found him on "Caring Bridge," an online support site for those suffering with cancer and other major illnesses. I sent him a note of encouragement and began to read his journaling of his battle with the disease. Kevin's posts, for the most part, were extremely upbeat and positive. There were, of course, the occasional writings where the reader could detect the tired and weary state he was in. Kevin stepped out of that cancer-ridden body on March 20, 2010 to receive his new, WHOLE body and take up residence in Heaven. It was exactly nine months before Robbie's passing.

At the end of December 2012, a year after Rob had passed away, I was sitting at my computer. All of a sudden, I heard the name, "Julie Walker." It was as if the Lord had spoken her name to me. I thought to myself, "Julie Walker? I'm not sure where she is. I just know they moved *somewhere* in

Colorado." I plugged Julie's name into a Facebook search. When the list of Julie Walker's in Colorado popped up, I recognized her picture immediately.

I sent her a message on Facebook, essentially saying I hoped that she and the kids were doing okay and I understood what she had been going through in dealing with the loss of Kevin. A few days later, Julie responded. She didn't know we had lost Robbie and said if I ever wanted to just "catch up" to give her a call.

I tried calling her, left a voice mail, then Julie called me back that night and we had an enjoyable visit. We began text conversations for a few weeks and then began to talk on the phone. A lot. Julie's sister and her family, including her mom, all live in the same area. In late February, she invited me to come for a visit in Colorado. I had been to the state on a few occasions like youth ski trips, etc. and always loved the mountains there. I excitedly accepted the invitation and made my plane reservations.

When Julie picked me up at the airport that Sunday morning, it was the first time we'd seen each other in TWENTY-FOUR years! It was a great trip and when it was over, we both knew God was up to something bigger than we imagined.

We carried on a long-distance relationship for the next year and half. How God blessed us during this time! On September 6, 2013 in Estes Park, Colorado, Julie and I were married. We now make our home in Monument, Colorado. She's a sign language interpreter and we now daily seek God's plan to use us for His glory, however He sees fit! (Traveling is NOT a problem!)

Regarding my kids, Rachael, is married to Michael Gorospe, and gave birth to our first grandson, Grant Michael, on November 29, 2013. They live in Jacksonville, Florida. Michael and Rachael both work for Florida Blue (formerly Blue Cross/Blue Shield). Reid married Brittany Morrow on Robbie's and my anniversary in 2011. I was blessed to conduct their wedding. They live east of Houston. Reid is an environmental engineer and Brittany is working on her masters/doctorate in psychology at the University of Houston. At the time of this writing they are awaiting the arrival of their first child, and our second grand-child. Atticus is expected to be here in early to mid-March.

Regarding Julie's children, Adrienne married Michael Anstice in June of 2013. Adrienne is a hair-stylist and Michael is a master's degree student, studying anthropology with the desire to become a college professor. At the time of this writing, they live in Denver, Colorado. Jared is currently studying orientation and mobility at the University of Northern Colorado in Greeley. He plans to work with the blind, helping them learn skills to navigate through life.

There's my life story up to now. Over the next several weeks, you'll be reading 42 of my memorable and amusing moments and you'll see for yourself why I have always said, "Life's an adventure! And I'm *Livin' It Up!*"

Robert Noland

Robert began his writing career as a songwriter, while working for 10 years touring in Christian music. He released his first series of Bible studies in 1988 and in 1991 began writing for a para-church student ministry. Noland has since authored over 50 titles spanning from children to adult audiences for denominations, faith-based organizations, Christian ministries, and publishers. His first book titled *The Knight's Code* was released in 2010 and he directs a men's ministry of the same name. Robert is now a free-lance writer, living in Franklin, Tennessee with his wife of 30 years and has two adult sons. Visit him at robertnoland.com.

Randy and Robert have been friends for many years, walking through much life and ministry together. This book brought yet another new and unique collaboration for their friendship.

Livin' It Up!
Published by Livin' It Up Ministries, Inc.
Monument, CO
In Cooperation with
517 Resources, Inc.
Franklin, TN
Copyright © 2014 Randy McLelland
Copyright © 2014 Robert Noland
Publishing, Cover & Interior Design: Elyon Media
www.elyonmediagroupllc.com
ISBN 978-0-578-14584-6

For more information, visit www.randymac.com

Mama and the UFO

In the early 70's, there was an epidemic of UFO sightings being reported. One such story came out of Calvert, Texas where my parents lived in a rural area, just off Highway 6. According to one report, in a pasture directly across the road from their house, a UFO got so close to the ground that the grass was burned in a round shape. News crews came and took pictures of the scorched patch of earth. After that initial flurry of attention, things quieted back down.

But awhile after that, my mom began to make reference, particularly in casual phone conversations, to her "friend." When questioned about it, she simply stated that she had seen a bright light flashing and hovering just above the highway, west of their house.

Mama had decided it was the UFO.

There was no sound of joking in her voice and she didn't seem concerned about it; evidently it didn't bother her; it was just there.

I suggested to her that the sighting was most likely a light from a nearby radio tower, but Mama was not buying it. Since she couldn't see it every night, how could it be just a tower light? She didn't consider, perhaps, there were some nights when fog or clouds might hinder her view of it.

That December, Robbie and I were going to visit Mom for a few days and I told my brothers that I was going to check out Mama's "friend" while we were there. One night she came in from the garage and reported, "He's out there." I walked outside and, sure enough, I saw the bright, white light flashing across the way. It was getting late, but I decided to drive that direction for a closer look.

Sure enough, there was the radio tower with the light attached. I pulled off on the shoulder of the highway, pulled out my video camera (way before smartphones), and began to record the tower. I figured I'd just get proof for Mama that I was, indeed, right.

Suddenly, everything around me lit up—VERY bright! I turned around to see the red and blue flashing lights on top of a police car and a spotlight fixed firmly on me, positioned by a now curious law officer.

There I stood in my T-shirt, plaid pajama pants, (yes, not just pajama pants, but plaid ones) and my slippers—shooting video of a flashing light! The policeman asked if everything was okay. I said, "Yes, sir. I'm just proving to my mom that this isn't a UFO." He asked who my mom was. I told him. He said he knew her. He told me to be careful and I assured him I would, as he got back in his cruiser and drove away.

I went back to the house and told Mama, "I have good news and bad news. The good news is, 'It's NOT a UFO.' The bad news ... your local police now know that you thought it was!"

After all, I couldn't go down by myself, could I?!

Now faith is confidence in what we hope for and assurance about what we do not see. —Hebrews 11:1 NIV

Isn't it interesting how we can be so sure that we have seen something that really isn't what we think it is at all, but equally as interesting that we can miss something that is so obviously there. Perception (how we process what we see) and perspective (the way we view something) are very important aspects of how we approach life and have a major impact on our faith.

Walking with Jesus Christ provides the right perception and perspective to every situation we can encounter, while sin can skew and distort how and what we see. That is why it is important to ask God daily for wisdom to see life through His eyes.

Dear Lord, help me today to see people the way you see them and situations the way you view them. Grow my faith as I learn to obey You. Help me to put my hope in You! Amen.

Wardrobe Malfunction

For several years, I have played the part of "Grandpa" in a Christian stage production called *The Promise* at an outdoor amphitheatre in Glen Rose, Texas. As you might imagine, doing a live play outdoors with a cast of about 100 people—and several live animals—can create some spontaneous and funny moments.

When I started my first season in the show, I was allowed to choose my own attire for the character. I picked overalls and a long-sleeved shirt. In the third season during one particular performance, I, along with the rest of the cast, knelt at the end of a scene where many folks, including "Jesus," were baptized. Seems there was a bit more water than normal on the stage at the end of that scene this particular night, and when I knelt, my left knee was in a puddle. No big deal.

But fast-forward a few scenes to the end of Act I where, once again, I, along with the rest of the cast, except Jesus, would kneel. That night, as I began to take the kneeling position, I noticed the wet denim of the left knee of my overalls was not sliding over my kneecap, but, instead, sticking tightly to it. And as my knee got closer to the concrete, I could feel substantial tension building in the fabric. And just as that knee touched the stage, those overalls ripped ... WIDE OPEN. I'm talking from just below the zipper on down—and around. There was now no tension in the overalls; it was all in my throat!

I'm kneeling there, my mind racing, and I have another hour of show to go. I spend a lot of time in the spotlight and much time sitting on a rock, facing the audience. And I had no spare overalls in the dressing room!

When the scene ended and we went to blackout for a 15-minute intermission, I rushed to the workroom where the costume coordinator was stationed. She was sewing when I ran in. I blurted out, "Christy, where's the duct tape?!" Without looking up, she pointed to a roll hanging on the wall. I grabbed it and took off for the men's restroom.

4

I sat there in the stall, my overalls down and turned inside-out, praying with each piece of tape that I applied, "Lord, PLEASE, let it stick!" ... Thank God for duct tape—and answered prayers. It held the overalls together.

I went to Wal-Mart, bright and early the next morning, to buy a new pair of overalls. As we were preparing for that night's presentation, one of the cast members asked me, "Randy Mac, did you buy an extra pair of overalls ... just in case?"

"Heck, no!" I told him. "Those things are thirty-two dollars a pair! I just bought another roll of duct tape."

When someone becomes a Christian, he becomes a brand new person inside. He is not the same anymore. A new life has begun! All these new things are from God who brought us back to himself through what Christ Jesus did. And God has given us the privilege of urging everyone to come into his favor and be reconciled to him. —2 Corinthians 5:17-18 TLB

Sin—disobedience to God—rips apart our lives and exposes our hearts to the world—like wearing a ripped pair of pants, standing on stage, in a crowded room; it can bring shame and insecurity. And sin costs us—dearly. But it cost God even more.

When we invite Christ to save us, He doesn't just give us a roll of duct tape and tell us to patch life up on our own—He gives us brand new clothes!

We can't, and we shouldn't try, to "get our life together" before we come to Jesus. That just doesn't work. He knows the mess we're in. He knows we're exposed and scared. He just wants us to come to Him in honesty and turn life over to Him. No duct tape, but a brand new start!

Heavenly Father, thank You that, in the Garden you saw Adam and Eve were naked and afraid, and while you could have destroyed them in Your judgment, You chose to clothe them out of love. Thank You that, through Jesus, I have an opportunity for new life and You choose to love me, even in my sin. Amen.

[If you are interested in knowing more about a relationship with Jesus Christ, turn to page 107 in the back of this book.]

In the Doghouse

Years ago, we had a couple of dogs. One was a bird dog I named Bone and the other one a half chow/half German Shepherd we had rescued from a shelter. We called him Hoover. Bone lived in a kennel, while Hoover ran free in our fenced-in back yard.

One weekend Robbie and I had to make a trip, so my in-laws came to take care of our kids, Rachael and Reid. When we got back home my father-in-law said, "Now, I like *that* dog," pointing toward Bone. "But, I don't like that one," he said, nodding in Hoover's direction. I asked why. He told me that anytime someone would go past our backyard, Hoover would bark non-stop. "It was just aggravating," my father-in-law said.

Right about that time ol' Hoover fired up, barking at a passer-by. I figured I would nip that behavior in the bud, so I grabbed my trusty "wrist-rocket" slingshot, along with one of those little ball bearing pieces of ammo. I loaded it into the leather and went out in the yard where Hoover was still barking through the fence. I drew back and let 'er fly. That dog went to howlin' and carrying on, as he ran around the backyard and finally hid behind the shed. "Lesson learned," I thought with pride.

The next morning I was out in the back yard and glanced across the way to my neighbor Mike's house. There in the driveway sat his van with a huge hole in the back glass. I remember thinking, "Hmmm ... I wonder what happened to Mike's van?" Then it hit me—a sudden, sinking feeling in the pit of my stomach. "Surely NOT," I thought.

I called Mike to ask about the hole. "Randy Mac, I have NO idea what happened," he answered, puzzled. "I came home for about ten minutes yesterday afternoon and when I got ready to back out of the driveway, I noticed the smashed window."

"Well, I can tell you what happened." Then I recounted the story.

Evidently my shot had gone over Hoover's head, but was close enough to scare him, thus making him howl and run. His noise was loud enough to cover the smash of my projectile, which had ricocheted off the road, crashing through Mike's back glass.

I called my friend, Bobby, at our local auto repair shop, described the van window, and he told me it would cost around $55.00 to install the replacement glass. I called Mike and told him to just run by Bobby's to get it fixed.

A while later, Bobby called. He said, "Hey, Randy Mac, that's privacy glass in that van." I asked what that meant. He said, "That means it's gonna cost $189.00!"

I paid Mike's $100 deductible and he turned it into his insurance company. From that moment to this day, I cringe every time I see a slingshot.

Give to everyone what you owe them: Pay your taxes and government fees to those who collect them, and give respect and honor to those who are in authority. Owe nothing to anyone—except for your obligation to love one another. If you love your neighbor, you will fulfill the requirements of God's law. —Romans 13:7-8 NLT

Isn't it amazing how our seemingly great ideas and good intentions can turn against us, and not only cost us, but also make us feel foolish? Like telling your neighbor you shot his back glass out with a slingshot, and costing nearly $200 to fix, is a far cry from a grand plan to teach the dog a lesson.

We are going to make mistakes—and big ones at times—but integrity and making things right can often overcome the poor decision. Doing the right thing when we mess up is, not only a witness to our faith, but a reflection of glory to God.

Dear Jesus, I know it's not if I will make a mistake, but when. Help me to pay attention and own up quickly to anything I do that is wrong or offensive. Teach me to grow in integrity and to always make things right with You and all those around me. Amen.

Week 1
Thursday

Where There's Smoke, There's Fire . . . Ants

When I was nine years old, my family moved to a community called "Old River," near the waterway of its namesake. While I had often watched my dad put out ant poison on a mound, I soon saw that these new folks had another way of controlling the fire ant population. And it was very impressive to me that fifth-graders could be so knowledgeable about such things.

I walked down to Wayne Follis' house to meet Donnie Knox and him. They were preparing to annihilate a rather large fire ant mound, right in the middle of the front yard. Seeing the gas can and book of matches made me know something exciting was about to happen! (Please, kids, do not try this—anywhere!)

I watched Wayne carefully douse gasoline all over the mound, and then pour a small trail from the mound, all the way over to the sidewalk by the garage. Everything was ready. Wayne struck one of those matches and lit the end of that gas. We watched as the fire made its way across the yard to the ants. WHOOSH!!! The mound was quickly and completely consumed in fire, and within a minute or two, the flames were gone—along with the ants.

I walked back to my house, marveling at my newfound knowledge. It was then that I remembered— there was an ant bed in MY yard! And now I knew exactly what to do and how to deal with them!

I got our gas can and found some matches. I saturated the bed—with way more gas than needed—and made a little trail of fuel across our yard. I lit a match and then dropped it on the gas trail. I watched the fire move toward the mound and just like at Wayne's house— WHOOSH!!! The mound went up in flames!

I didn't think about the fact that the ants at MY house had built their mound against a pine tree. Also I didn't know that pinesap was flammable, but I learned quickly. I knew that, at any moment, my dad would be coming home from work. I figured he'd be less than happy to find one of our big trees up in smoke. I ran to the barn, got a tow sack, and proceeded to beat out the flames.

Looking back, I guess I could have told my dad those ants started the fire ... after all they were FIRE ants! ... But thinking back, it's probably best I didn't.

Temptation comes from our own desires, which entice us and drag us away. These desires give birth to sinful actions. And when sin is allowed to grow, it gives birth to death. —James 1:14-15 NLT

Sin is a lot like setting a fire outside. Once it's burning, the fire is in control, not us, and can destroy things.

Is there any place in your life where you have a "gas can and a book of matches" in your hand and you know it's dangerous territory? It may be something no one knows about it yet. Consider the consequences that you cannot know right now—before you strike the match, so to speak.

Is there an area where you are being tempted to "set a fire?" Today's verse would be a great one to memorize for moral protection. And maybe my fire ant story will come to mind the next time you're struggling with temptation too!

Savior, even though I know that fire burns, I have been burned so many times. Help me as I grow, to sin less, obey You more, and hurt no one. Amen.

Discomfort in Coach

A couple of years ago I was invited to speak at a church event in McComb, Mississippi. The nearest city that Southwest Airlines could get me to was New Orleans. So, I left my house early that morning to make my way to Love Field in Dallas. I didn't take time to eat breakfast at home, so before I left Glen Rose, I stopped and got a breakfast croissant and a cup of coffee. I enjoyed it as I headed north.

After I got to the airport, parked, and through the checkpoints, I guess we were somewhere near the halfway mark in our flight to New Orleans when I felt the need to stretch. There's not a lot of room in those airplane seats, especially when you're a big guy with a window on one side and a fellow passenger on the other. I slowly and cautiously reached my arms straight up over my head.

Then I felt a yawn coming on, so I brought my left hand down to cover my mouth. As my hand brushed over my mustache, I felt something that didn't feel like facial hair. I quickly turned my head toward the window, trying to locate the object. Somehow, and obviously unbeknownst to me, when I was eating that croissant on my way to the airport, a rather large ball of cheese had become affixed to my facial hair.

I immediately began to recount the number of people I had close interaction with since eating my breakfast in the car. There was the lady who checked my baggage. She didn't tell me. There was the lady who scrutinized my driver's license and boarding pass, making sure I was the guy on the license. She could have said, "Oh, you didn't have the cheese in *this* picture." But she said nothing. There were the crewmembers that greeted me as I boarded the plane, the attendant who brought my coffee, and the fellow passenger, whom I had been visiting with, who was sitting on the cheesy side of my mustache.

I'm quite sure, by the size of that cheese ball, that most, if not all of those people, had noticed it. And, since it didn't really go with what I was wearing, they probably knew I hadn't hung it there on purpose. Yet nobody told me.

I've had others explain to me that the reason people don't often tell us things like that is because they don't want us to feel embarrassed. Oh yeah ... *please* don't embarrass me. Let me go ahead and see another thousand or so people with a gooey cheese ball hanging from my face. Surely I'll find it that night when I'm brushing my teeth before I go to bed. And certainly I'd feel no embarrassment at that point!

My brothers and sisters, if one of you should wander from the truth and someone should bring him back, remember this: Whoever turns a sinner from the error of his way will save him from death and cover over a multitude of sins. — James 5:19-20 NIV

The principle of this story is, so often as people, we tend to "look the other way" or "choose to not get involved." As Christians, Scripture is clear that we are involved already! God wants to make us a part of His business—and His business is people. Helping others, even if and when it makes us uncomfortable, is what we do as His followers.

If you ever see someone with cheese on their mustache, just kindly, quietly call it to their attention. But more importantly, if you see someone wandering from God's way, go after him/her to say how much He loves and wants the person back in His fold. God is in the saving work and we are His workers!

Lord God, help me to make Your business my business, but to stay out of the things that aren't Your business! Help me to help people. Lead me to be honest and gentle in all my ways. Amen.

The Wedding Trip

Over these many years that I've been in ministry, I've sung at a lot of weddings. Several years ago, some of our good friends were getting married in the church where we had all attended for quite a while. (That's an important detail to the story.)

The couple asked me to sing two songs during the ceremony and I was, of course, honored to be a part. It would be the first time that I would ever sing "The Lord's Prayer"—a beautiful song, which I'm sure for many singers is not difficult, but it was a good stretch for me, since I have always leaned more toward hymns and Southern Gospel music. It seemed that in no time the big day had arrived and I was nervous about the songs.

The wedding ceremony was scheduled to start at seven o'clock. Of course, everyone who is in the wedding is expected to arrive early. That's so the bride can be sure that the bride's maids are all ready with their hair done up and everything in place, that the groom is actually on the premises, and none of the groomsmen forgot their tuxedos or brought the wrong shoes.

Although often stressful, weddings are always very exciting events. As for me, there's always plenty of time to walk around and get nervous. And this night was no different. With only a few minutes until show time, I was getting a bit panicked, mulling "The Lord's Prayer" over and over in my mind. Then I had the strangest feeling come over me that my tie was probably not straight.

I walked into a room behind the pulpit area, thinking there would probably be a mirror there. None. I walked into another room. No mirror. Knowing we couldn't be far from seven o'clock by now, I ran upstairs to yet another room. I couldn't believe that there were no mirrors to be found! Then I noticed a light on in a room at the other end of a long, dark hallway. Maybe *there*, I thought. I walked very quickly down that dark corridor ... and fell right into the baptistery.

14

If you're not well versed with church buildings, it's like a small indoor swimming pool. But—thank the Lord—it was empty. If there was going to be a baptism the next morning, it would have been full of water, and I would have been sunk. (Pun intended.)

While I didn't actually fall down, I did make a lot of noise bouncing down the four steps to the bottom. And I'm sure people on the other side of that curtain, waiting on the wedding to begin, were wondering, "WHAT was THAT?!" Grateful to have no broken bones or torn clothing, I stopped worrying about my tie, went out, and sang my songs. At least now I knew exactly where the baptistery was in my own church ... but I still had no idea where the mirrors were!

For the Lord grants wisdom! From his mouth come knowledge and understanding. He grants a treasure of common sense to the honest. He is a shield to those who walk with integrity. He guards the paths of the just and protects those who are faithful to him. Then you will understand what is right, just, and fair, and you will find the right way to go. For wisdom will enter your heart, and knowledge will fill you with joy. Wise choices will watch over you. Understanding will keep you safe. —*Proverbs 2:6-11 NLT*

Notice the phrases "guards the paths of the just," "protects those who are faithful to him," and "you will find the right way to go." The pattern here is that God wants to help us walk down the road of life successfully.

We are going to have lots of stumbles and falls from unseen drop-offs and pitfalls in the road ahead, but the key is staying on God's path—day in and day out—focused on Him, not ourselves.

What path are you on today? Where are you headed? Is it dark where you're walking? What do you do, where do you turn, when you fall down? The road God offers doesn't guarantee an easy life, but it does provide His care and protection every step of the way.

Take a minute and write down in the margin of this book the promises that God makes us in today's passage.

And one last piece of advice from me ... don't run down dark hallways—even in churches!

15

Dear God, it is so comforting that You can see behind me, beside me, and in front of me. Guide me today. Guard me today. Help me to follow You wherever You lead. It may not always be easy, but it will always be the best place for me to be. Amen.

Week 2
Monday

Blunder to Wonder

A trip to a nursing home can make for an unpredictable and sometimes uneasy adventure. While serving as a youth minister years ago in east Texas, I decided it would be good for our youth group to serve the elderly. We made plans on this "ministry mission" to go to a local nursing home on a Sunday afternoon.

The kids gathered at the church and climbed on board the bus for the short trip. As we drove, I tried to put them at ease. I talked through some of the things they may experience—like folks reaching out to touch them, asking for help to get them out, etc. I told the kids that all they needed to do was smile, make polite conversation, and just be nice. And then I said something that, in retrospect, would have been wiser for me to leave un-said, "If you don't know what to do—just watch ME."

We got to the nursing home and made our way into the large gathering area where many of the residents were spending the afternoon. Some were watching TV, some working puzzles, some visiting with friends, and some were just sitting quietly. Very quickly the students had taken their places—backs against the walls around the perimeter of the room. They were, just as I had instructed, watching me! So, it was time for me to show them how it's done.

I was working the room, just chatting with the residents, exchanging pleasantries. Things were going well. Then I spotted one lady sitting in the middle of a sofa by herself. She was slumped back, slid down, with her arms folded across her mid-section. She was wearing one of those knee-length "dusters" and a pair of white bobby socks—and no shoes. She was also sporting a very large frown, so she became my next target of encouragement.

I walked over, stood in front of her, smiled, and asked, "How are YOU today?" She just glared at me. I tried again, as if she didn't hear me the first time, "You doin' okay today?" She continued to glare. I smiled, reached down, and patted her gently on one of her hands, and said, "You have a great day!" As I did, she threw her arms apart, as if to communicate, "Don't TOUCH me!" The glare was now even more intense. I decided my ministry in THAT part of the room was done and I turned away.

As I stepped away from the couch, that lady put a hand down on each side of her bottom, pushed herself up, and kicked me—solidly—right square in the rear with her right bobby-socked foot! I KNOW it was the right one, because when I turned around, that leg was still suspended in the air.

My youth group was watching me. I had told them to. From then on it was more difficult to rally a group of students for an outing to the nursing home.

There is a story in the New Testament where some men decided to do some ministry too, but they got a little more than a kick in the pants. Check out this passage in Acts 19:13-16.

Some Jews who went around driving out evil spirits tried to invoke the name of the Lord Jesus over those who were demon-possessed. They would say, "In the name of Jesus, whom Paul preaches, I command you to come out." Seven sons of Sceva, a Jewish chief priest, were doing this. One day the evil spirit answered them, "Jesus I know, and I know about Paul, but who are you?" Then the man who had the evil spirit jumped on them and overpowered them all. He gave them such a beating that they ran out of the house naked and bleeding. NIV

We can, all too often, have the best intentions when we begin to try and help people, but regardless, there are times it can backfire—badly. God has an odd way of accomplishing wonder from our blunder. Let's look at what happened in verses 17-20 when this story spread around the community.

When this became known to the Jews and Greeks living in Ephesus, they were all seized with fear, and the name of the

Lord Jesus was held in high honor. Many of those who believed now came and openly confessed their evil deeds. A number who had practiced sorcery brought their scrolls together and burned them publicly. When they calculated the value of the scrolls, the total came to fifty thousand drachmas. In this way the word of the Lord spread widely and grew in power. NIV

The sovereignty of God changes everything. He can redeem any situation—turn it from bad to—God. Blunder to wonder!

We are going to have crazy, even embarrassing, moments in life, there's no way around that. And walking with the Lord is no guarantee that life won't kick you when you're not looking, but trust that He can make miracles from mistakes. And that is what makes life in Christ such an adventure!

Father, I know You can use anything, anytime, anywhere. Help me to learn from my mistakes and use them for Your glory, but also use me to show Your wonder to the world! Amen.

Fangs a Lot!

Sometimes the fact that *my* life is an adventure seems to mean that those around me are going to inherit it too. It was especially challenging for my wife, Robbie, because she had to live with me!

Some years ago, I was invited to speak at a high school commencement in New Mexico where a friend of ours was the principal. Robbie and I flew from Dallas to Amarillo and then made the short drive into New Mexico for the event. While there, one of my buddy's friends learned that a hobby of mine is making good use of rattlesnakes. I make jewelry from their vertebrae, tan the snake hides for hat bands, belts, etc., and, of course, eating the meat when the snake is large enough and fresh enough.

This friend had a whole (deceased) rattlesnake in his freezer and offered it to me. How could I turn him down? I called Southwest Airlines and explained my potential carry-on baggage. They approved it; we were good-to-go.

Since the drive back to the Amarillo airport was relatively brief, the flight to Dallas was very short, and the trip back to Glen Rose was quick, the snake was still frozen when we got home. So, I just put it out in our garage freezer. (I had a "bottom-shelf agreement" with Robbie.)

A couple of weeks later, I was at home working on the computer when I remembered my frozen, fanged friend. So I brought it in the house, filled our kitchen sink with hot water, took the still-coiled snake from the bag, and placed it in the water. The snake began to float and I went back to work at the computer.

A few minutes later, Robbie walked up behind me, leaned down, and, rather quietly, said, "I just wish you would *tell* me when I'm going to walk in the kitchen and find a rattlesnake floating in the sink!"

Scripture often refers to Satan as a serpent or snake. Romans 16:19b-20 says, *"but I want you to be wise about what is good, and innocent about what is evil. The God of peace will soon crush Satan under your feet. The grace of our Lord Jesus be with you." NIV*

Now, Robbie, obviously, had been around snakes more than the average woman, so she was not prone to screaming and running when she encountered one. But she *was* a woman, and a snake *is* a snake, and it *was* in *her* house, in *her* sink. She wasn't overly startled, because of her familiarity with my "hobby." She had gotten wise to the fact that a rattlesnake may be in the house at any given time—warning or no warning.

The Bible teaches us from cover to cover that we must always be aware, on guard, alert, and "be wise." We shouldn't get so familiar with evil that it no longer bothers us.

Is there anything in your life right now that truly is evil, but you are growing more and more accustomed to its presence? Don't be fooled. The enemy is a master of luring us into a trap by having us walk in and close the door on ourselves.

Today, take a good, long look at your life. Is there an activity you wouldn't even consider inviting Jesus to join you in? A person you wouldn't consider inviting Him to meet? A place you wouldn't invite Him to go with you?

Maybe it's time to "get the snake out of the sink."

Dear Jesus, I confess that _____ can lead me away from You and toward sin. Please help me in this area. Don't let me get used to evil anywhere in my life. Give me eyes to see and ears to hear You. Amen.

Hide and Go ... Call 9-1-1!

Many of the adventures in life as parents come from raising our kids. Robbie and I were blessed with two wonderful children, Rachael and Reid, who are today grown and married adults. Rachael is now a mom herself, which, of course, makes me a very proud grandpa.

In the summer of 1986, we had moved to Haskell, Texas for me to take my first full-time youth pastor position there at First Baptist Church. Rachael was a toddler and Reid was still a baby. Haskell is a small town, about fifty miles north of Abilene, completely surrounded by cotton fields. Our first house was a small, stucco one, situated on an alley, just one block off the main highway running through town.

It was during the first couple of months there that Robbie and I had taken the kids to do some shopping. We got home and were in the process of bringing in all the groceries. Reid was crawling around the house and Rachael was running in and out of the back door. After a few minutes, Robbie and I realized we'd not seen Rachael for a bit.

Rob called out to her. ... No answer. Another call went out. ... Still no answer. By now, we were both yelling her name—in the house and out in the yard. Rachael was nowhere to be found. Our sudden fear was that someone had turned off the main road, come down the alley, and taken her from the yard. Robbie was crying and my stomach was in a knot as I called our local police and sheriff departments.

After I had given them all of the required information and knew they were on the way, we continued our search. I remember—as if it were yesterday—walking with Robbie through our small living room and hearing a tiny voice from underneath my roll-top desk say, "Daaaaddddy ... you didn't look under heeee-rrrre!"

Rachael had crawled under the desk and pulled the chair back into place, for an impromptu, very quiet game of hide-and-seek. She started working her way out from under the desk. As she appeared, Rob was softly repeating to me, "She doesn't understand. She doesn't understand." I think Rob thought I was going to bust her bottom, but I was just fighting back the tears and ready for a hug!

I thank God for my kids who, to this day and after all these years, help me to live it up!

He doesn't play hide-and-seek with us. He's not remote; he's near. —Acts 17:27 MSG

Hiding is only fun when everyone is in on the game. It can be sheer terror for someone that's not privy to the playing. Hiding started very early on in human history, in fact, in the Garden of Eden. After Adam and Eve realized they had disobeyed God, they hid. Only Adam did not want God to *ever* find him, because he thought the Creator was about to make his brand new species extinct!

But God first called out to Adam to come out. "Adam, where are you?" He knew where they were. (Remember—He's God.) When they came out, God covered them and then the entire plan of salvation began to unfold. At that moment, Jesus was on the way! It was just a matter of time.

Are you hiding from something today? Has something shamed you, and even though you may be around people, in your heart, you're hiding who you truly are. Know today that, just like I was ready to hug my now-found daughter, not punish her, God, just as in the Garden, is ready to help get things right and draw you close.

God is a good Father ready to restore and heal anything that makes us want to hide. It's not a game to Him either. He is seeking; it's time to be found.

Father God, thank You that I don't have to hide anything from You. Help me today to draw near to You. Help me to be exactly who You have made me to be. Amen.

[Remember to turn to page 107 if you would like to know more about having relationship with God.]

Week 2
Thursday

Hide the Ham! I'm on the Lam!

When we were young, my brothers—Charles and Richard—and I would often spend a week or two in Arkansas with some of my dad's family. Part of our time was spent with my grandmother, whom we called … wait for it … "Mama Goose." The rest of it was spent on the hog farm with our Aunt Mary Ethel and Uncle Carter. While they had horses, mules, chickens, turkeys, goats, and cattle, the hogs were their main source of income. And during our visits, we "got" to help take care of the animals.

I learned early on that hogs are needy critters … and nasty … and they smell bad. (Of course that all changes once in the form of bacon, sausage, or ham cooking in a skillet.)

One day, there I was outside just doing boy stuff— huntin' birds with my BB gun, chasing cats, etc. I looked out into the small pasture in front of the barn and saw some of the hogs circled up, eating corn that my uncle had poured on the ground for them. I started throwing rocks up into the air to see how close I could get to the hogs. Well, I got REAL close. In fact, I nailed one.

I chunked a rock up, watched it come down, and then saw a BIG sow's front knees buckle. She went completely down and rolled to her side. I just KNEW I had killed her. And I KNEW Uncle Carter was gonna be REAL mad. So I ran around to the front yard. I figured that maybe he would just think the sow had died of a heat stroke in the Arkansas summer.

A bit later I peeked around the house and, to my relief, realized the hog was up and about. I had just "cold-cocked" her with that rock. I love bacon, but I didn't want to get it that way!

We know that our old sinful selves were crucified with Christ so that sin might lose its power in our lives. We are no longer slaves to sin. For when we died with Christ we were set free from the power of sin. —Romans 6:6-7 NLT

From young to old, when we realize we have done something horribly wrong, we become slaves to both the sin and the consequence. What might happen to us, or how someone will respond to us, becomes the focus of our lives once we've committed an offense.

In this story, the hog woke up and was fine, ending my slavery to this situation. But for me, it was just a matter of time until something else happened!

That's why Jesus came—to free us from sin, shame, guilt, and condemnation. He won't change consequences that we put into motion, but He will stop the condemnation that we place on our hearts. That's a real game changer for our souls.

Today, thank Jesus for the freedom from the bondage of sin and shame; then thank Him for His grace, mercy, and forgiveness.

Lord Jesus, thank You for the freedom You alone can give. Thank You for Your grace, mercy, and forgiveness through Your sacrifice for me on the cross. Amen.

Through Fire & Flood

Not long out of high school, I went to work in the industrial area along the Houston Ship Channel. I was what you'd call "green" or inexperienced. I worked each day in a fabricating shop with a handful of welders and pipefitters. I was most interested in welding and some of the older guys would, on occasion, let me try my hand on some minor projects—ones that didn't need to look real nice when completed.

One of my friends and mentors was a guy named "Joe." Joe was good at what he did. He was doing some work on a catwalk—a footpath constructed of angle iron and grating, oftentimes mounted on the outer perimeters of the upper levels of buildings, storage tanks, etc. Joe decided this would be a good project for me to get some experience on, so he loaned me his welding hood and gloves to let me give it a shot.

I remember very well, upon completion of one weld, Joe examined my work and declared, "That's a 'gorilla weld.'" I asked what that meant. "Strong, but ugly," he said.

Joe could take a torch and cut a piece of steel plate with an edge so smooth that it would look like it had been cut with scissors. I was impressed. I asked him how to do that. He gave very simple instructions: "Hold your breath, just like you do when aiming a rifle." Sounded easy, so I gave it a try.

Joe let me use his cutting torch, which was an honor in itself, because those guys were VERY particular about the use and care of their tools of the trade. I laid a piece of steel plate on the work table, drew a straight line with the soapstone, donned the dark cutting goggles and gloves, and fired up that torch. I drew a deep breath, held it, and began to cut.

As I started cutting, Joe leaned over and calmly said, "Hey, Randy." I was focused, so I didn't respond. Again, he said, with no excitement in his voice at all, "Hey, Randy." I was getting a bit perturbed, trying to make a

26

smooth cut. Once again he said, "Hey, Randy." As the cut piece fell to the floor, I pulled the goggles off and said, "WHAT, Joe?!" He pointed down toward the floor and said, "Your pants are on fire."

An ember had fallen and taken lodging in a wrinkle just above the hem of my blue jeans. Since I had boots on, I had no idea that about five inches of denim was already gone as the flame continued to climb. I reached down and slapped the fire out. I remember Joe just standing there with a cup of coffee, grinning.

Shortly before dawn Jesus went out to them, walking on the lake. When the disciples saw him walking on the lake, they were terrified. "It's a ghost," they said, and cried out in fear. But Jesus immediately said to them: "Take courage! It is I. Don't be afraid." "Lord, if it's you," Peter replied, "tell me to come to you on the water." "Come," he said. Then Peter got down out of the boat, walked on the water and came toward Jesus. But when he saw the wind, he was afraid and, beginning to sink, cried out, "Lord, save me! Immediately Jesus reached out his hand and caught him. — Matthew 14:25-31a NIV

Like my pants catching on fire when all I wanted to do was cut metal, and Peter sinking, thinking he was going to drown when all he wanted to do was go to Jesus, there are going to be those moments when our best plans backfire on us.

Listening intently to God, as well as to those that He has placed around us for counsel and wisdom, is crucial to finding success in life—and avoiding wildfires and high water!

Heavenly Father, help me today to keep my eyes on You and You alone. Guide me in Your ways and Your wisdom. Amen.

Week 2
The Weekend

Helen's All-You-Can-Eat Buffet

Serving on staff as a minister in Texas means you're going to get invited to eat at many meals. And it just so happens that I don't mind eating at all!

Also, I have been known to take in verbal information and then convince myself that I can remember the details without recording the info anywhere. More than once, this has caused a debacle in my scheduling ... and my life. So it was on one spring day.

One of the sweet, elderly ladies in our church had recently experienced her husband's passing and was really having a difficult time adjusting to life without him. She invited my wife and I over to her home for lunch on a weekday. I accepted the invitation. I didn't tell anyone. I didn't write it down.

The lunch date rolled around and at noon, I made the short drive back to our house for lunch. My wife, Robbie, had cooked a wonderful meal and I ate up. I enjoyed it so much that, the best I can remember, I had seconds of everything on the table. After finishing off my plate, I made my way to our den and my easy chair, knowing I had ample time to kick back for a snooze before returning to the church office.

Just as I leaned back in my chair, the phone rang. I answered. It was Helen. She very softly asked, "Randy, are y'all still coming over for lunch?" What was I to do?! Knowing her emotional state, I certainly couldn't say, "Sorry, Helen. I forgot." So instead, I said, "Yes, ma'am! We are just about to leave to come over!" I quickly explained to Robbie and we jumped in the car. Soon, we were sitting at Helen's house ... for lunch ... again.

As you might expect, Helen had also prepared a wonderful—large—meal. Food was all over the table as we sat down, trying as best we could to act hungry. Everyone knew Robbie wasn't a big eater so small portions on her plate seemed natural. But Helen had seen me eat meals at the church. She knew I loved good cooking. I remember consuming the first round and then Helen handed me the bowl of mashed potatoes. "Have some more," she said.

"There's plenty!" What was I to do? Again, knowing her emotional state, I surely couldn't say, "Oh, no ma'am. I've had enough." So instead I said, "Thanks!" and ate another round. The meal was capped off with dessert and coffee.

I remember leaving Helen's house that day in a carbohydrate fog, feeling extremely uncomfortable, and now no time for a nap. It made for an interesting afternoon. But Helen was happy. And that was all that mattered.

Learn to do good, to be fair, and to help the poor, the fatherless, and widows. —Isaiah 1:17 TLB

There are multiple places in Scripture where we are commanded to care for widows and orphans. Those left in vulnerable situations clearly have God's attention, therefore He asks us to give them our attention.

In our busy, crazy lives, let's pay attention to those that most people do not see. Watch for the people Jesus would want us to love on—like He would.

Today's Scripture says we must "learn to do good and to be fair and to help" those less fortunate as ourselves. Isn't it funny that we have to learn that lesson and keep learning it? And it would even help if I wrote it down!

Father God, teach me to see those that You see—even those who may be invisible to so many. Help me to slow down and love people the way You would. Amen.

Week 3
Monday

All Systems Are ... Go!

I grew up next door to the Hutter family. Sid was the oldest of the kids and one of my best friends growing up. We spent a lot of time together.

We were about 11 or so when I spent the night at their house on this particular Friday night. We stayed up late watching scary shows like "Alfred Hitchcock" and "The Twilight Zone," and playing "Monopoly." Still we were up early that next morning, watching "Tarzan" on "Jungle Theater." Now *those* were the days! Watching shows like that can make a couple of eleven-year-old boys mighty hungry. And so we decided to go find something to eat.

The Hutters had a big, walk-in pantry. I distinctly remember both of us looking around in that huge space for something to fill our own void. Sid's mom worked during the week and Saturday was her day to sleep in. We knew it'd be best to not wake her up and we were big enough to take care of ourselves, at least when it came to eatin'.

My eyes made their way up to the top shelf, where I saw several boxes of cereal. Ahhhh, breakfast! I reached up and grabbed a box. The only cereal in the box was that piece or two that somehow gets down between the inner bag and the box. So I grabbed another box. Same thing. For some reason when the Hutter kids emptied a box of cereal, instead of putting it in the trash, they put it back on the shelf. And so the search continued for something to satisfy our nagging hunger.

Finally, we spotted it—a big, ol' box of Del Monte prunes. We grabbed them and headed back to the den to watch more Tarzan. We sat there in the floor, starin' at the TV, and eatin' prunes ... all of 'em ... the whole box.

Funny the things we learn when we're young. Until that morning I really didn't know much about prunes; didn't know what they were made of and didn't know they could be used for "medicinal purposes"; but I learned real quick.

And Sid and I didn't see much of each other for the rest of that day. We were, as they say, indisposed.

"I have the right to do anything," you say—but not everything is beneficial. "I have the right to do anything"—but not everything is constructive. —1 Corinthians 10:23 NIV

We've all heard the old saying, "Too much of a good thing." It's funny that the sentence doesn't even have to be finished. We know what it means. Life is all about balance. We spend our lives trying to find the right amount of love, money, time, words, and on and on the struggle goes.

Is there any area of life where you're out of balance? Somewhere you know too much is happening? Maybe somewhere else that it's not enough? The balance to life is only found in one place—a daily relationship with Jesus Christ. He knows how much is enough and how to make up for a deficit or a surplus.

Just because we have the right to eat "the whole box" of anything in life does not mean that we should!

Lord, lead me to balance in every area of my life, for You alone know what is right and best for me. Amen.

Shootin' & Fishin'

I grew up hunting ducks, dove, squirrels, rabbits, and deer. When I started dating Robbie, I was introduced to the world of quail hunting. In the early days, about the only time I got a chance to hunt quail was on the occasional trip to my in-law's farm in Mills County, Texas. But when we moved to Haskell, Texas, I could drive to a friend's pasture with my dog and be looking for birds in about ten minutes.

After we'd been there for about three years, our pastor resigned to move to another church. A few months later, we were blessed with a new pastor and his wife, Brother Jim and Sammie Turner. He was also a quail hunter and we enjoyed many trips to the fields in search of a covey or two.

One day, Brother Jim and I were in my office swapping hunting stories of days gone by. He proceeded to tell me of the time that he and his son were hunting in a field near Rising Star, Texas on a cold, blustery day. He said they happened up on a big covey of birds that were huddled behind an old Model A car fender, using it as a wind break. Brother Jim recounted how they shot into the birds and bagged some thirteen or fourteen. This set me off.

"You shot them on the GROUND?!?!", I asked, as if in shock. "You're not supposed to shoot ducks on the water, doves in a tree, and you're not supposed to shoot quail on the ground!" I proclaimed, rather forcefully. He just laughed at me and said, "Yeah! You call that a 'skillet-shot.'" Well, I was quite riled up and he loved it.

A few days later I was sitting on the back row in our fellowship hall during our monthly deacons meeting. These meetings were scheduled right before the Sunday evening church service. Brother Jim was talking to the men about the importance of personal evangelism. In so doing, he made this quote. "Men, it's a lot like quail hunting. You gotta get 'em one at a time." About the time he said that, his eyes met mine. I think I saw a bit of fear, but I grinned and held my tongue. (Which in THIS case was mighty hard to do.) I'm sure he was thankful I did.

After that meeting I told him I wasn't going to be in church that evening. With a puzzled look, he asked why. I responded, "I looked at the convenience store across the street and saw a bunch of teenagers hanging around the parking lot. I'm pretty sure some of them need to hear about Jesus, so I'm gonna walk over there and get me a 'skillet-shot!'"

One day as Jesus was walking along the shores of the Sea of Galilee, he saw Simon and his brother Andrew fishing with nets, for they were commercial fishermen. Jesus called out to them, "Come, follow me! And I will make you fishermen for the souls of men!" At once they left their nets and went along with him. —Mark 1:16-18 TLB

Year after year, decade after decade, statistics tell us that the primary way people come to know Christ as Savior and Lord is through a personal relationship with a Christ-follower. While we all would love to have the gift of preaching to thousands and seeing hundreds respond, the majority of us just need to focus on the handful that we will encounter today and be "Jesus" to them. The old adage, "You are the only Bible some people will ever read," is just as true today as ever.

Whether you call it "fishing" like Jesus did or "hunting" like Brother Jim, the "catch" still comes one at a time! Share Jesus today with everyone you come into contact with by a warm smile, a friendly word, or a testimony of what He has done for you.

Father, today, may I be kind, loving, caring, and reflect Your character that is alive in my heart. Give me the boldness to share You anywhere I can. Amen.

Week 3
Wednesday

The Pancake Principle

Since I'm an early-morning riser, breakfast has always been an important part of my day. For many years, I've enjoyed cooking the "first meal" for others—or just for me. I can pretty well "whup up" a morning feast consisting of any of the typical breakfast foods, but one of my favorites have always been pancakes. So as you might suspect, here's a couple of pancake stories ...

Once, while hosting a radio show in the Abilene area, I had to read a public service announcement about a particular civic group that was having a pancake supper fundraiser. As I read the notice, the idea came to me that I should interject a little humor at the end. I announced to the listeners, "Next time you're making pancakes, try putting about a third of a cup of un-popped popcorn in the batter. It really won't affect the flavor, but the pancakes WILL turn themselves over."

In a few minutes, the call-in line lit up. A sweet lady on the other end apologized for bothering me, but said that she was trying to get ready for church, had missed part of the recipe, and asked me to repeat it for her. (I told her it was just a joke and that it would most likely mess up her vent-a-hood!)

Another morning a few years back, I wondered if I could make a pancake on the carafe warming plate of our drip coffee maker. I placed a drop of water on the burner and when it danced around before vanishing, I knew it was the proper temperature. PLUS it was the perfect shape and size for a pancake! I got out the mix, stirred it up, and poured it onto the coffee maker's warmer.

Now, if you make pancakes, you know that when the middle bubble breaks, it's time to turn the pancake over. When the middle bubble broke on this particular pancake and it was time to turn it over, I realized that to do so, I'd have to turn the whole coffeemaker over! I learned that day there's no Teflon on a coffee maker's carafe warmer ... and I was REALLY glad Robbie stayed asleep while I cleaned up the mess!

Jesus answered, "I am the way and the truth and the life. No one comes to the Father except through me. —John 14:6 NIV

It's hard to improve on the pancake, isn't it? It's such a simple, easy, tasty breakfast food. No matter how creative a cook may get, whether you're a chef or a kid, there's really just one way to make pancakes. You can try and add to the recipe or change your cooking method, but it's hard to improve the simplicity of the batter and butter on a griddle.

Mankind has come up with literally thousands of ways to try and find salvation. But there is only one way and today's simple, easy verse spells it out clearly. Jesus is it. He's the only way. You can try all kinds of roads and paths, but there's only one to Heaven.

So, what's The Pancake Principle? Some of life's simple, unchanging truths just need to stay simple and unchanged, because they work perfectly just like they are.

Creator God, Thank You for making a simple way for me to get to You. While it was so difficult for You to sacrifice Your Son, that act of love made a Way for me to find salvation forever. Thank You. Amen.

[For more info about a relationship with Jesus Christ, turn to page 107.]

35

Week 3
Thursday

You Can Hide the Skunk, but not the Stank!

One hot, September day when I was a sophomore in high school, I was in woodworking class and needed to ask my shop teacher a question. I walked outside to find Mr. Harvey spraying a water hose. As I walked up, he said, "Randy, I smell a skunk." Pointing towards a fifty-five gallon drum next to the building, I said, "There's a tail right there." He sprayed it with the water hose and out ran the baby skunk it was attached to. I had always wanted a pet skunk and quickly surmised this was my opportunity!

Knowing "baby" skunks can't spray yet and after much pleading, Mr. Harvey gave me the okay to catch it. I crawled up under the pipe, grabbed the little critter by the tail, dropped her into a brown paper sack, and rolled the top down.

After shop class, I went back over to the main building to get ready for last period—P.E. I stopped by and put the sack in my bottom locker with my football gear and headed to the gym. A bit later, my buddy, Mack Jones, walked into the locker room and said, "Your skunk just sprayed." I replied, "No, she didn't." "Step out in the hall," Mack quipped. I did. I sniffed. It wasn't good.

The stench had already begun wafting through the halls of our small high school via the central air system. The entire girls' typing class was outside, doubled over and gagging. This feeling of intense heat started going through my body. As I walked back into the locker room, I remember thinking, "I'm about to be in BIG trouble."

Within minutes, I heard those little flush-mount ceiling speakers pop, indicating that an announcement was about to be made. I distinctly remember the voice of Mrs. Orms, the principal's secretary, as she simply said, "Randy McLelland, come to the office, please." I was pretty sure that life was about to change, if not end completely.

When I got to the office, she said, "Mr. Womack (the principal) wants to see you at your locker." When I walked around the corner, there, sitting in the floor, was one of our lady custodians—with a BIG can of aerosol fragrance—holding her nose and spraying my locker. Mr.

Womack looked at me, grinned a little (I think), and said, "Boy, don't choo know bettuh than to put a skunk in yuh OWN locka?" (I reckon it would have smelled better in someone else's locker.)

Then Joshua said to Achan, "My son, give glory to the Lord, the God of Israel, and honor him. Tell me what you have done; do not hide it from me." Achan replied, "It is true! I have sinned against the Lord, the God of Israel. This is what I have done: When I saw in the plunder a beautiful robe from Babylonia, two hundred shekels of silver and a bar of gold weighing fifty shekels, I coveted them and took them. They are hidden in the ground inside my tent, with the silver underneath." So Joshua sent messengers, and they ran to the tent, and there it was, hidden in his tent, with the silver underneath. They took the things from the tent, brought them to Joshua and all the Israelites and spread them out before the Lord. Then Joshua, together with all Israel, took Achan son of Zerah, the silver, the robe, the gold bar, his sons and daughters, his cattle, donkeys and sheep, his tent and all that he had, to the Valley of Achor. Joshua said, "Why have you brought this trouble on us? The Lord will bring trouble on you today."
—Joshua 7:19-25a NIV

Trying to conceal disobedience in our hearts is a lot like trying to hide a skunk in your locker. It will only work for so long before everyone knows the truth ... and that always stinks.

Keeping your list of sins short is important to a healthy spiritual walk. Regularly and quickly confess any known sin to God. Waiting and keeping it hidden away just causes trouble for us and those we care about.

Heavenly Father, help me to be honest with You and with others when I make a mistake. Help me not to hide or try and disguise my sin, but own up to it, ask for forgiveness, and move on to what You have next for me. Amen.

Week 3
Friday

The Root of the Problem

When I played football as a kid, I was informed that I was "all thumbs." I have also determined that neither of my thumbs—or however many I have—is "green," as they say. If you have a living plant that needs to be put out of its misery, but you just don't have the heart to do it, just bring it to me.

My lack of knowledge in caring for plants started becoming obvious when I was in high school. I remember well, one cool, autumn afternoon down in southeast Texas where I grew up, when we were out of school for the Thanksgiving holidays.

My dad was a shift-worker and was not home that particular day. My mom passed his instructions on to me that I was to get the leaves and pine straw raked and bagged up. She added that the chore would have to be done before I could go do anything else.

So right after lunch, I got started, working with much gusto and quickly getting the leaves and straw into plastic trash bags. I decided that I would REALLY surprise my mom by going the extra mile.

The flowerbed across the front of our house was full of some kind of dead sticks. They were ugly and I knew that mom would be so pleased if I got rid of them all. I worked quickly so that I could get done before she walked back outside. I didn't want to spoil my surprise for her.

The sticks easily came out of the ground, as I pulled each of them out. In no time at all, I had that flowerbed back to clean, level dirt—ready for new plants. I then asked mom to step outside. I was so excited for her to see my hard work.

She took one look and screamed, "WHAT HAVE YOU DONE?!" It turned out those "dead sticks" were some kind of flowering plant that came back to life every spring.

Today, in front of my own house, there are several shrubs. They've been there for about ten years and are now very brown. Someone told me they're dead and that I need

38

to remove them. I'm thinkin' that maybe I better wait until Spring ... just to be sure.

Everything that happens in this world happens at the time God chooses. He sets the time for birth and the time for death,the time for planting and the time for pulling up, the time for killing and the time for healing,the time for tearing down and the time for building. —Ecclesiastes 3:1-3 GNT

We tend to learn in two different ways—first, from making mistakes—and second, from being patient, waiting, and watching for God's timing. Acting too quickly or waiting too long can hurt us. Timing is everything. Today, lean on the One Who created life, its rhythms and patterns. Listen to Him for the right time "to plant or to pull up."

Creator God, thank You that You know all things because You made everything. From the people I'm with, to the work I do, to the thoughts I have; help me to listen to You for what to do and when to act. Amen.

Week 3
The Weekend

Righteousness & Reid's Rear-End

As kids, my two older brothers and I were never beaten, but our parents did subscribe to the idea that a bit of "heat" properly applied to the back, lower region of the body would provide encouragement to make better choices in the future. For us—it worked. And I remembered that when I became a daddy.

Rachael, my daughter, was easily corrected most of the time. If we just *looked* at her like we were upset, she'd go to pieces. Not true of Reid, my son. That boy was one of those "strong-willed" ones that I always heard Dr. James Dobson talk about on his Christian psychology radio program. So, Reid got his share of "bustin's" during his early years.

Since you never knew when there was going to be a need for a paddle, I made three of them. Nice ones. Out of 1 x 4 lumber. I'd cut 'em to length, carve out a nice handle, and round down the edges and corners. There was one under the seat of the car, one under the seat of the suburban, and one between the refrigerator and microwave.

One day when Reid was about four, he was out with me in my shop. He did something he shouldn't have done and I gave him a warning, "Boy, you do that again and I'm gonna tear your bottom up!" Almost immediately, he did it again. I've always believed you should never make a promise you don't plan to deliver on, so I took Reid by the hand, led him into the house, grabbed the paddle from between the refrigerator and microwave, and gave him three or four swats. He cried out and ran into his bedroom, as usual.

Typically, after a paddling, Reid would go to his room, cry for a few minutes, come out, and get busy with life again. But today was different. After several minutes, he was still in his room. I peeked around the door to see him on the bottom bunk, his face buried in his pillow. He was trembling and sobbing. I had never seen him do this before, so I walked into his room and sat down on the edge of the bed. Rubbing his back, I asked, "Son, what's the matter?"

I remember so vividly him raising his head off that pillow, turning to look at me with that tear-streaked face, and asking, "*Is it* torn up?" Even though the pain was gone, as children can often do, he imagined his bottom was literally torn up and he was too afraid to look at it.

Now an adult, Reid is MUCH bigger and I'm sure he could dismantle me if he chose to do so. We have a great relationship and many times, in my Father's Day card, he thanks me for those "bustin's" during those early years that helped make him the man he is today.

My son, do not despise the Lord's discipline, and do not resent his rebuke, because the Lord disciplines those he loves, as a father the son he delights in. —Proverbs 3:11-12 NIV

It's easy for us as adults to think that discipline ends at childhood, but God the Father will teach us through correction until we go home to be with Him. He allows us to suffer consequences of poor choices; He can delay a blessing until we are ready to receive it; He can make us wait until our growth catches up with our assignment. His actions are always about the best for us, because of His great love for us. But, assuming you're much like me, we tend to learn more from burdens than blessings, from problems than peace.

Dear Father, help me to remember that when you discipline me, it is not a sign of judgment or condemnation, but love and protection. Help me to trust Your heart and Your timing in my life. Amen.

Week 4
Monday

Say What?!

If I take a Benedryl, you better point me to a place where I can lay down. I'll see you in about eight hours, because I just can't handle the stuff. In fact, while I can drink a pot of coffee, go to bed, fall asleep in minutes, and slumber peacefully all night, there are some meds that will knock me out completely. But . . . even worse, the ones that cause me to appear as though I'm awake, while, in reality, my brain has slipped into a state of cobwebiness (pronounced cob-web-e-ness). A zombie-like state might be another apt description. The lights are on, but nobody's home. KnowhutImean?

Many years ago when I was a youth minister, I woke up with severe tension in my neck muscles, a result of an injury I got at youth camp. We had some kind of muscle relaxers and the normal dose was two pills. I decided to take just half of one to try and get some relief for my ... uh, pain in the neck. Then I went on to the church to work.

About a half hour later, I was sitting in my office and one of my youth volunteers walked in to discuss the details of that night's youth gathering. He asked me a question and I tried to answer. I'm not even sure how to spell what came out of my mouth. Something like, "Weth...I thiiiink whath weeeeel do thooo moothic and den weel do thum grooop sthudy............"

I can still remember the look of confusion on his face and then he started laughing. I also recall him yelling out to everyone else on the staff, "Hey! Y'all come in here and talk to Randy Mac! Listen to this!"

My office was soon packed with people, taking turns asking me questions, and enjoying the conversation at my expense.

By around lunchtime, the medicine finally got out of my system. I had two thoughts. The first one was how glad I was that I didn't take a whole pill! And the second — don't ever take even half of a muscle relaxer again! Or with me, it would sound more like "muzzle reelaazer."

Therefore, with minds that are alert and fully sober, set your hope on the grace to be brought to you when Jesus Christ is revealed at his coming. — 1 Peter 1:13 NIV

For the message of the cross is foolishness to those who are perishing, but to us who are being saved it is the power of God. — 1 Corinthians 1:18 NIV

When we don't yet understand the grace and mercy of God, someone speaking of Him or showing His love can sound a lot like me on muscle relaxers. We hear the person speaking, but the language just doesn't make any sense. But when God opens our heart through His Spirit, the words are understood and the message is clear. The language of God can sound foolish until someone interprets His meaning.

When I was sitting in the church office "under the influence," I was uttering nonsense, which made my communication just babble to those around me. But hours later back in my right mind, I was teaching students the Word of God, fully understood.

What "language" are you speaking to those around you? Is it just foolish talk or the words of faith? Is it gibberish or Jesus? Let's stay alert and speak the message of the cross by the power of God. And leave the interpretation up to God.

Lord Jesus, fix my mind on You, so I can make the most sense possible to those around me. Help me to communicate Your grace and love to others, whether they believe it is foolishness or salvation. Amen.

Week 4
Tuesday

Tee Time With Mr. Knox

When I was around nine years old, we moved to a neighborhood where everyone's house was sitting on two acres. There was lots of room between homes.

I was about twelve when the "golf bug" hit my buddies and me. We all went to Gibson's Discount Center and bought one golf club each—a 5-iron or a 7-iron—and a sleeve of three Arnold Palmer golf balls.

We made up a "three hole golf course" which, incidentally, didn't have any actual holes. We'd start from the Follis' mailbox and hit to the Sullivan's pine tree (next door). You had to hit the trunk of the tree below the lowest limb for the "hole." From there we'd hit way down, across the road to a post in our yard, and then work on the longest hole from my yard, all the way back to the Follis' mail box. We had a lot of fun and spent many summer hours out on the "course."

One day, Frankie Sullivan's grandpa gave him a full set of golf clubs. We'd never seen so many! Frankie and I were playing a round and he had already hit his ball from the pine tree in his yard towards the post in mine. He was out on the road when I teed up my ball. I hollered and asked him, "What's a 9-iron do?" He yelled back, "You just hit the ball as hard as you always do, but it goes higher, so it won't go so far." I decided that was just the club I needed.

As I hit that ball hard—and sliced it, I saw it veer to the right, but then lost sight of it. A few seconds later, I heard a loud "THUMP." I knew from Frankie's vantage point that he was able to see the ball. I hollered again and asked him what the ball hit.

He said, with his long, southern drawl, "Mister Knox."

I said, "Nuh-uh. It hit something metal."

Frankie countered, "Hit him first."

Mr. and Mrs. Knox, our neighbors across the street, were sitting in their lawn chairs out in the yard. My golf ball had come down and hit Mr. Knox upside the head, then

44

bounced off and hit his truck. We hurried over to check on him. With a cold rag to his head and me on the brink of tears, Mr. Knox kept assuring me that he was all right.

Mrs. Knox said that when the ball hit him, both Mr. Knox and his chair just fell smooth over. I still try to play golf occasionally. But I still can't bring myself to hit with a 9-iron.

Peter also knew what it was like to swing a piece of metal and hurt someone. But he carried something a little sharper than a golf club!

When Jesus' followers saw what was going to happen, they said, "Lord, should we strike with our swords?" And one of them struck the servant of the high priest, cutting off his right ear. But Jesus answered, "No more of this!" And he touched the man's ear and healed him. —Luke 22:49-51 NIV

Whether it's a golf club in the hands of a kid or a weapon in the hand of a man, all too often, as sinners, we can "shoot first and ask questions later"—which usually leads to someone getting hurt.

Submit yourself to the Lord daily and ask for wisdom in all your relationships. Always be someone who gives life and hope, never pain or hurt. Accidents will happen, but we can sure swing some hurt on people when we aren't careful. Today, be a blessing to everyone you meet and, if you're going to play golf ... be careful.

Lord God, thank You that You can help me avoid hurting people, intentionally or accidently. Help me to be Your vessel of love and care. Thank You for Your healing hand of mercy. Amen.

Week 4
Wednesday

Scoop. Poop? Oops!

In the late 80s while at First Baptist, Haskell, Texas, the pastor asked me to take over the "Kid's Time" children's message on Sunday mornings during the service. On some Sundays, I would use an idea from a book; other times, my creative juices would flow with an original idea.

I decided that on one particular Sunday, I was going to teach the children what's on the inside of us will come out when life "squeezes" us. I went to the store and bought a lemon, lime, orange, grapefruit, and a bag of grapes. I would have bought just one grape, but the folks at the store might have thought me to be strange. (Some of them thought me strange anyway.)

So that Sunday morning before church, I cut the little tip off the end of that lemon and, with a spoon, proceeded to dig all of the insides out. Then I filled it full of peanut butter and stuck the little tip back on the bottom. I put all of the fruit in a large plastic bowl and headed for church.

When "Kids' Time" rolled around during the worship service that morning, I made my way to the front with the children. I sat on the edge of the platform; they sat all around me on the floor. I put the bowl in my lap and began my incredible lesson.

I asked, "Boys and girls, if I squeeze this grapefruit reeeeeal hard, what's gonna come out of it?" "GRAPEFRUIT JUICE!" they called out. I crushed the grapefruit, letting the juice run into the bowl.

"What about this lime?" I asked. "LIME JUICE!" they answered back excitedly.
Then I crushed the lime the same way.

I did this same thing with each of the other pieces of fruit, saving that lemon for last. But now it was time for the BIG finish.

I held up the lemon and asked, "What should come out when I squeeze this lemon? "LEMON JUICE!" the kids hollered out.

I thought to myself, "I've got 'em now!"

Unfortunately, it never occurred to me what peanut butter would look like oozing out of that little hole on the bottom of the lemon when I squeezed it. Think about that for a minute. Picture it. I sure wish I would have. The kids were amazed, but I lost the adults.

Then I made a note to myself: When preparing an object lesson for children, always rehearse first to make sure it's appropriate for church!

Every tree is known by the fruit it bears; you do not pick figs from thorn bushes or gather grapes from bramble bushes. A good person brings good out of the treasure of good things in his heart; a bad person brings bad out of his treasure of bad things. For the mouth speaks what the heart is full of. —Luke 6:44-45 GNT

If we're all honest, there are plenty of times we get squeezed by stress or fear and, well, our lives look like peanut butter oozing out of a lemon. It just ain't pretty!

The more we cooperate with God's Spirit to change us into His image, the better chance we have of the world seeing Jesus when we're squeezed. Today, when you're met with your first challenge or temptation, let the "good things" of God be your choice and what you call on, to carry on, to come out.

Holy Spirit, help me to choose the good You offer when I'm faced with challenges. May Your treasure be my choice. May my mouth speak of You, as my heart seeks You. Amen.

Week 4
Thursday

My Mama, Yo Mama

My mom, now gone on to be with the Lord, was one of those women who loved her kids deeply. She would do anything to help us, sacrificing much along the way. We laughed a lot too. We had many fun times, as Mom would haul us kids and our buddies to the skating rink, bowling alley, swimming pool, fishing hole, and on and on. And if our friends were still with us at dinnertime, they were always welcome at our table.

Mom also understood the need for firm discipline. If the violation wasn't too flagrant, you might get a warning—but just one. As I remember, they often went like this, "You do that again—you better make sure your heart belongs to God, 'cause your butt's gonna be mine." (Please don't be offended by that word, but "rear" in this instance just doesn't get the job done.) While we did choose wrong over right at times, Mama made sure we knew the difference.

My dad was a shift worker, so there were many Sundays he wasn't able to go to Sunday school and church. But Mom made sure my two brothers and I were there. I can still remember as an eight-year-old boy, tugging on Mama's dress sleeve during the invitation on a Sunday morning in that big church in Pasadena, Texas, telling her "I need to go down there and talk to Brother Joe." The Lord saved me that morning.

Her children praise her, and with great pride her husband says, "There are many good women, but you are the best!" Charm can be deceiving, and beauty fades away,but a womanwho honors the Lord deserves to be praised. Show her respect—praise her in public for what she has done. — Proverbs 31:28-31 CEV

My two wonderful children, Rachael and Reid, are both Christians today. Their mama taught them much about the Lord, too. I'm now a granddad and I know my daughter and daughter-in-law will carry on the proud tradition of their mothers.

If you had a Christ-like mother, honor her memory. If you have one, thank her. If you are one, bless you! I thank God for godly mamas.

[For your prayer today, thank God for your own mom and her place in your life. Also pray for the other mothers in your family today.]

Mistaken Identity?

One Friday night, not long after I had graduated from high school, a couple of my buddies, Robert and Ronnie, invited me to go to Baytown just to cruise around. Baytown was the closest "big city," about fifteen miles from where we lived. I accepted their offer. But I also took along a rubber mask I owned that looked like a scary old man.

As soon as we got to Baytown, I slipped the mask on in the car. We made a quick stop at the Jack-in-the-Box drive-thru where we got a lot of laughs from the people sitting inside. We left there and made our way onto Texas Avenue, better known as "the drag," where people cruised up and down. There was a car full of girls stopped at the intersection. Their windows were down. So was mine. I stuck my head out of the window and my tongue out of the mask. I still remember their screams as we drove past.

One of the guys said, "I dare you to walk IN to Jack-in-the-Box with that mask on." We knew everyone who worked there, so how could I turn down such a challenge? We walked into the restaurant and everyone was cracking up. Everyone, that is, except the policeman who was eating his burger. He just chewed and stared. I walked over to him and said, "It's just a mask." He said, "Ya wanna take it off?" "Should I?" I quizzed. "I think you better," he responded. Now I really *was* the center of attention.

As the policeman started getting up, I thought he'd never stop coming out of that booth to finally stand up. He was huge! And he now had the floor. With everyone watching in total silence, he poked me in the chest and growled, "How'd you like to have a .357 magnum right there?" I answered him very honestly, "I wouldn't like that at *all*." As he swallowed his last bite of burger, he was now ready to chew on me. And he did. Thoroughly.

I finally realized he wasn't as mad as he was concerned about my intention. I apologized and I also may have offered to shine his shoes or something. Finally he lightened up, so I asked him if it was okay to drive down Texas Avenue with the mask on. He quipped, "Son, you can *streak* down Texas Avenue with it on! Just don't go into a place of business wearing a mask ever again!"

Love others well, and don't hide behind a mask; love authentically. Despise evil; pursue what is good as if your life depends on it. —Romans 12:9 (Voice)

While this is certainly a funny story from my youth, the end proves that masks make us uncomfortable. Even on Halloween when it's expected, they can be creepy. You can't really know who is behind them and it's hard to tell someone's facial expressions or intentions. And lots of horror movies involve a mask!

One of the great by-products of Christianity is Jesus tells us who we are and that we have no need for masks anymore. We don't have to disguise ourselves. We are accepted, loved, and He offers us His own identity for security and safety.

Is there any situation where you tend to put on a mask? Is there any person you feel you have to put on a fake front or disguise for? Know today you are accepted and loved by Jesus—exactly the way you are.

Lord, thank You for giving us a new identity in You, one where we are safe from anything the world might throw our way. Help me to be who You made me to be. If I'm wearing a mask anywhere, show me, so I can remove it and never wear it again. Amen.

Week 4
The Weekend

Just a Plane Faux Pas

Some years ago, I had to make a quick trip, flying from Abilene to Dallas in the morning and returning in the afternoon. Back in the days before 9-11, there was a small airline called The Dallas Express. The plane only had about twenty seats. In a short time, one could, if one so chose, get to know most, if not all, of their fellow passengers. You can guess the choice I made.

As I started my return trip at Love Field, I was making my way to the gate when I noticed a lady dragging (yes, literally) a large suitcase across the carpet en route to the baggage check-in point. I offered to help her and she agreed.

We struck up a conversation there in the airport, so after boarding, we ended up sitting across the aisle from each other. As no surprise to those who know me, we began to talk about food and recipes, then wild game and, of course—road-kill—my specialty. (Brings a whole new meaning to a chef saying, "Bam!")

I began sharing some of my stories about eating armadillo, coon, rattlesnake, squirrel, bobcat, and the like. I was clear that anything found dead on the roadside was considered a potential meal for me. As I began to elaborate and expound on my unique recipes, I explained there are some general "rules of thumb" in regard to picking up road-kill.

First, Rule #1: NEVER fight a buzzard.

Rule #2: When traveling in the winter, keep a can of white spray paint in your trunk. I explained, "If you're making a winter road trip with plans to return the next day—every time you come to a dead animal in the road, jump out, and spray a white ring around it. Next day on your way home, any dead animal *not* in a white circle is FRESH!"

Time flew as I educated this nice lady in road-kill skills. Before long we were on the ground, taxiing to the terminal in Abilene. I had mentioned to my new friend that I was a Baptist youth minister, but realized I had never asked what she did for a living. So, I did. She smiled and answered, "I'm a rabbi."

It was at that moment I realized I had just explained, all the way from Dallas to Abilene, how to cook and eat any and all dead animals found on the roadside to a woman who must follow the strict dietary laws of the Jewish Torah.

Therefore let us stop passing judgment on one another. Instead, make up your mind not to put any stumbling block or obstacle in the way of a brother or sister. I am convinced, being fully persuaded in the Lord Jesus, that nothing is unclean in itself. But if anyone regards something as unclean, then for that person it is unclean. — Romans 14:13-14 NIV

Context is everything. Perspective is important. The wonderful Jewish lady and I had a great time talking about road-kill. To be honest, I think she was a bit intrigued by the subject. No one was offended; in fact, we had a good time. And, to her credit, she never became defensive or decided to "teach me a lesson" from the Law either.

Paul is telling us in this passage from Romans, as he often did, that we need to stay focused on the prize and not so much on the details that separate us. And that prize is Jesus and the goal is leading people to Him.

Heavenly Father, help me to stop looking at labels and look at lives—lives you died to save. Strengthen me to be bold for You, yet gentle as You. Help me to never cause anyone to stumble, but to be a pathway to You for others. Amen.

Week 5
Monday

Litterin' in the Lincoln

I've driven older vehicles my entire life. My dad always said, "As soon as you drive a new car off the lot, it's a used car." But when you drive older cars, you come to expect from time to time, you are going to have to deal with breakdowns. And the first sign of an impending problem is usually a funny noise from your car.

On a crisp fall morning a few years ago, I had plans to meet my good friend, Casey, at a Cracker Barrel for breakfast located in between my house and his. As a rule, we met there around 8:30 a.m. And, also as a rule, I'm always ten minutes late. But I had decided this day was going to be different! I planned to leave in plenty of time to fill that ol' Lincoln Town Car up with gas and beat Casey to the Cracker Barrel. I couldn't wait to see his face when he walked in and saw me sitting at that table, already drinking coffee.

Before daybreak, I backed out of my driveway and started down the street. Immediately, there was a huge noise coming from the car. I had never heard anything quite like it. I couldn't pinpoint exactly where the racket was coming from, but I felt a sick feeling come over me, familiar I suppose to those of us who drive older vehicles. I was thinking, "Whatever this is, it sounds REAL bad." But the car seemed to be running okay, so I drove the short distance around to the E-Z Mart, where I could at least try and see what the problem was.

I pulled up to the gas pump under the light. I saw my friend, Angela the store clerk, standing just outside the glass door with a funny look on her face. As soon as I got out of my car, she announced, "You have a trash bag stuck underneath your car." I walked around to the passenger side to see what she saw. And she was right.

54

Just a few minutes before leaving the house, I had put our garbage out for pick-up ... on the driveway ... behind the car. When I backed out, I snagged one very large bag with the end of my bumper. I looked behind my car to see a steady stream of trash all the way out to the main street. But it didn't stop there. There was garbage all along the street coming into our subdivision, leading all the way back to our house. I picked up trash for half an hour before the mess was cleaned up.

I was late again to meet Casey at the Cracker Barrel. And Angela at the E-Z Mart still laughs every time she sees me.

Therefore, since we are surrounded by such a great cloud of witnesses, let us throw off everything that hinders and the sin that so easily entangles. And let us run with perseverance the race marked out for us... —Hebrews 12:1 NIV

It's ironic that when we are dragging our personal baggage around, everyone seems to see it but us. We can get so accustomed to and "entangled" in our own sin that we just hear the noise it makes, while ignoring the trail of trash we leave behind us.

Is it time to clean up a mess you've been dragging around for far too long? Is there anything you need to "throw off" that is just hindering you from running the race and living the life Jesus has for you? He knows exactly what to do with your sin and just wants you to agree with Him about it, so He can forgive you and move on in the relationship. Freedom can be yours today. Just decide you're going to take out the trash.

Father God, thank You for making provision for my sin and forgiving me. Help me to stay sensitive to Your Spirit when You convict me of my wrongs. I want to stay free and following after You. Amen.

Week 5
Tuesday

Life in the Fast Lane

Some years ago, I had been invited to entertain at a banquet for a civic group in a neighboring town. Often these events were held in the large room at the Cliff House restaurant, about fifteen miles south of the town where we lived. I had written on my calendar this location and the start time of the event.

Since the sponsor had told me this was to be a rather small gathering, it would not require that I bring any sound equipment, and thus it would not be necessary for me to arrive much more than a few minutes early. I walked into the restaurant, guitar case in hand, about ten minutes before 7:00 p.m. As I entered, I told the man behind the register that I was there for the banquet. He said, "There's no banquet here tonight." An immediate uneasiness came over me. Did I have the wrong day? What happened?

I called the gentleman whose name and number I had written on my planning calendar. He informed me that the banquet was at the Stamford Country Club. I didn't even know Stamford *had* a country club. But they did ... on the other side of town. Now I was in a race against the clock.

As I put the pedal to the metal, frustrated with myself for now being late, I came up behind two little elderly ladies who were obviously not running late to their destination—or anywhere for that matter! I never noticed the driver looking in the mirror to see there was someone behind her, needing by. My frustration escalated, my impatience grew. Finally, I came to a passing lane and flew past the little ladies.

I made it to the banquet about ten minutes late. I decided in my performance that I would share with the folks the now funny story of me going to the wrong place for the banquet. I also decided to tell them that I might have actually made it on time had it not been for these two little old ladies, poking along through town. Everyone laughed and I moved on with the program.

Afterwards, many nice people lined up to speak kind words to me about the entertainment. I took the hand of one sweet lady, smiled at her, and waited for the compliments. She looked me square in the eyes and said, "Hello. I was one of the little old ladies you were trying to pass on the way here."

The man of few words and settled mind is wise; therefore, even a fool is thought to be wise when he is silent. It pays him to keep his mouth shut. —Proverbs 17:27-28 TLB

To be honest, I'm paid to open my mouth—to preach, speak, share, sing, and even tell jokes. But, regardless of our personality, gifts, and skills, teaching the brain to engage before the tongue can be a tough lesson to learn. Putting the brakes on, before the truck backs up with the words flowing out, is a challenge. I know it is for me at least.

While my story is funny and the little lady forgave me—I think—our words can certainly cause others a lot of pain, if we aren't careful. And then, in reality, that hurts us, as well as our reputation.

Consistently committing our mouths to Jesus can be just as important as our hearts, because "out of the mouth the heart speaks." (Luke 6:45) Today, remember—as I will too—that our mouth and heart are connected and allows people to see Jesus in both.

Lord Jesus, settle my mind and guard my tongue. Teach me when to speak and when to be silent. Let me be someone who blesses people with my heart and my words. Speak to me—and through me—today. Amen.

Week 5
Wednesday

Eggs-plosion!

It gets really hot in Prescott, Arkansas. On one steamy afternoon there, my Aunt Mary Ethel gave my cousin Riley and me, both of us around 10 or 11 years old, the job of "robbing" a turkey nest, taking the eggs down the road, and throwing them out in the pasture. She told us the eggs were not fertilized, and that the hen, not knowing of this situation, would "sit herself to death trying to hatch them." If Aunt Mary Ethel was trying to help the turkey, then we would to. So Riley and I formulated a plan, but we were both rookies at this job.

The nest was in a brushy thicket, right next to a wooden fence at the edge of the pasture. Riley climbed on the fence with a long stick and I took my place on my hands and knees at the bottom. He would reach down through the brush with the stick and poke the hen, which would make her jump up and off the nest for a minute. With each poke and subsequent jumping up of the hen, I'd reach under the fence, grab an egg, and put it in a shoebox. We became a lean, mean egg-snatching machine. In a matter of minutes, we had successfully removed all of them from the nest and *that* part of the job was done. Now it was time for phase two—egg tossing.

Riley and I took the eggs down that hot, red-gravel road some fifty yards or so. He took the first one out of the box and prepared to launch it into the pasture. I told him to wait—that we should break the first egg very gently, just in case Aunt Mary Ethel was mistaken and there really was a baby turkey inside. He walked up to a fence post, then looked back at me and said, "Here. Y*ou* do it. I'll hit it too hard."

I took the egg, reached down, and picked up a small rock from the road. Holding it, rather close to my face, I began to gently peck on the shell. It was, at that moment in time, that I learned the hard way that an unfertilized egg, when exposed to excess heat over several days, will rot. I also learned that a rotten egg produces a gas, which produces internal pressure. And I learned that with only a small amount of pecking with a rock, a rotten egg explodes. A runny purple and green liquid ran down my face. I won't speak of the aroma, but it was not of this world.

I ran back to Aunt Mary Ethel's house, laughing as I *ex*haled, then gagging as I *in*haled. I spent the next hour scrubbing with Lava soap and dousing myself with my Uncle Carter's cologne.

Something about the combination of Lava soap, men's cologne, and rotten turkey eggs made others not want to sit with me at suppertime. And I never questioned Aunt Mary Ethel's knowledge of turkeys and their eggs again.

Pay attention to advice and accept correction, so you can live sensibly. —Proverbs 19:20 CEV

Without good advice everything goes wrong— it takes careful planning for things to go right. —Proverbs 15:22 CEV

When you take matters into your own hands and end up with rotten egg on your face—and sitting alone at supper—you start to pay attention to those who know better than you. As we get older, it also gets easier to stop listening, to not pay attention, and not carefully plan. But good advice will always be good advice. And sensible living is always the best choice.

God's Word is ever available and always true, no matter our age, situation, or problem. We can look to Scripture in any setting for any solution. If the direct answer isn't there, the principle for a wise choice will be.

Connecting daily to God through His Word, as you have been going through this book, will keep you from a stinkin' life *and* keep egg off your face.

The Bible—Read it. Believe it. Trust it. Live it.

God, You are the Author of Life, therefore You know what is best in every situation. Lead me back to Your Word daily. Teach me Your ways. Help me to pay attention, accept correction, live sensibly, and plan carefully by listening to You. Amen.

Burned Into My Memory

I will never go through any holiday season that involves fireworks that I won't recall a particular night at the house of a buddy of mine named David. His family lived just off the highway. David's dad was a rice farmer and their home set back off the road a bit. Although "cherry bombs" had been declared illegal for the average novice pyro-technician, the rather large explosives were made available to farmers to drive the destructive "rice birds" from their fields. His dad had a whole case of them. David asked if I'd like to "chunk" some, as we used to say. Of course, I couldn't pass up such a great opportunity.

We didn't have a "punk" to light the fuses, so David got a mosquito coil out of the garage. They're the shape of a burner on an electric stove, and, when lit, smolder very slowly, giving off some serious smoky pesticide designed to keep mosquitoes—and most everything else—away from the area. (This was well before the invention of citronella.)

We did light up the sky and were able to discharge several cherry bombs before the coil was gone. But there were still some in the box, so David went to his dad's car and retrieved one of those big, ol' "It's-a-Boy" cigars from the glove compartment. And so the show went on.

David was always the curious type and began to question just how much gunpowder was packed into a single cherry bomb. We decided to cut one open to see. There was quite a bit of powder and David poured the silver-gray contents on the sidewalk beside the house. He knelt down, turned his head away, closed his eyes, and stuck the hot cigar into the pile. There was a huge flash and it was pretty impressive. David wanted to see it, too, so we cut another bomb open. With another heap of gunpowder on the concrete, David handed me the cigar and stepped away, waiting for me to ignite it. I knelt down, turned my head, closed my eyes, and stuck the cigar into the powder. Nothing happened. I tried a few more times, still nothing. David was always pretty sharp, so he informed me that I needed to puff the cigar to get it red-hot and then try again. … So I did.

I had no idea that a rather significant amount of gunpowder had stuck to the end of that cigar during my initial attempts to light it. When I sucked on that cigar, there was a sudden, large flash in front of my face, burning my fingers, eyebrows, any near-by hair, and glazing the lenses of my glasses. I still remember David laughing and hollering, "That was cool!" He said during the flash that my eyes got huge! I'm pretty sure they were too.

I've not seen a cherry bomb since that night, and, really … that's alright with me.

Being rubbed in the dirt can teach us a lesson; we can also learn from insults and hard knocks. —Lamentations 3:29-30 CEV

We have all heard the phrase, "He (or she) had to learn 'the hard way.'" We've all had to learn this many times on many fronts. We can hear fire is hot and listen to stories about people who have been burned, but most of us still have to see for ourselves. And that's why it's called sin, by the way.

God is a loving Father Who gives us chance after chance to get it. But a loving father also knows his child has to fully understand to be able to mature and grow. Where is God trying to get something across to you "the easy way?" Is he knocking on your door, letting you know in a gentle way that something needs to change? Why not listen to Him today before life blows up in your face or your whole life flashes before your eyes?!

Father God, thank You that You want me to get it the easy way before life gets hard. Help me to see when You are trying to get my attention. Help me to listen to Your voice and follow You. Amen.

Week 5
Friday

Sound Effects

Some of my adventures have caused excitement not only in my own life, but also in the lives of others. Sometimes it's on purpose, but other times, completely unintentional. That pattern started early though.

Around the age of seven, I was invited to go with our neighbors down to Chinquapin, Texas. It's in the south Texas coastal area around Matagorda Bay. I've never been certain exactly what the correct pronunciation is, but we always just said it to sound like "Chinky-pin."

Our neighbors had a cabin right at the water's edge. We always had fun making the 100-mile journey south, spending a couple of days of fishing for speckled trout in the bay and catching blue crabs right off the pier behind the cabin. But this particular trip was not one for fun.

The Morse's had a daughter, Susie, who was my age and one of my best friends. There were some repairs needed at the cabin and Susie's dad, Ernie, or "Uncle Ernie" as we called him, was going down for just the afternoon. Susie and her mom were going as well, so I was invited to tag along.

Although I never saw one in my visits to "Chinky-pin," we were told there were rattlesnakes in the area, so we should be cautious. This was, of course, several years before I began to hunt and catch rattlesnakes. In fact, this was before I knew there really are some *good* snakes!

The country roads there were made with shale rock and nut-grass grew down the middle of them. Anytime we were walking on those roads we were given strict orders not to walk in the grass, but to stay on the shale, because the snakes may be hiding in the grassy cover. I also didn't yet know that some people are extremely afraid of snakes. Uncle Ernie was one of those people—also something I did not yet know.

Back in the '60's, aluminum drinking tumblers were very common. They came in a variety of colors and, since they were unbreakable, were really convenient to have around places like their cabin. Susie's mom had made some

Kool-Aid and we were drinking out of those tumblers. They always had crushed ice at the cabin and I've always been an ice eater. Uncle Ernie had crawled up under the cabin to work on a water leak. Susie and I were just hanging around beside the house, waiting for him to get through with the repairs and come out.

I had finished all my Kool-Aid and was in the process of finishing off the last of my crushed ice. A small clump of it had gotten stuck in the bottom of my cup. So I shook that tumbler real fast to loosen the ice. What I didn't know was, to someone underneath a cabin in the dark, crushed ice shaking in an aluminum tumbler strongly resembles the sound of a "buzzing" rattlesnake.

I'm still not sure how he did it, but while I remember it took Uncle Ernie several minutes to crawl up *under* that cabin, it seemed that he was floating on air as, in a matter of seconds, he shot back *out*.

I can't remember exactly what he said, but I do remember him stuttering as he tried to talk after figuring out there wasn't a snake after all. But—I figured I might better slither out of his way for a bit anyway.

But whoever listens to me will live in safety and be at ease, without fear of harm. —Proverbs 1:33 NIV

On any given day, we hear a lot of "noise" in our lives that causes us to fear. And there are times when that fear overwhelms us and causes us to react in ways that hurt ourselves, as well as others. It is ironic, however, that the vast majority of our fears never come true. We waste much time and energy on concerns that never come to pass. What we think we heard turned out to be just another noise. Just like the ice in my tumbler.

What are you afraid of today? What is worrying you? Could it be you're only hearing noise that isn't actually a threat to you at all?

What's the answer for curbing the fear? Listening to the Lord. Read and re-read today's verse. Ask God to make it very real to you. His voice can calm our hearts and speak over all the noise of the world, as well as our fear.

Father God, help me to focus and listen to You today. Help me to trust that You will help me to live in safety. Calm my fears and put my heart at ease in Your peace. Amen.

Week 5
The Weekend

The Gospel According to SPAM

A while back, I had joined a networking group and was blessed there with a lot of new friends. One of those new buddies was Lora. At the first meeting I attended where she was present, she introduced herself as "your party girl." I quickly learned that what she meant was she was a representative for a jewelry company known as *Silpada*. The company makes very nice silver jewelry and Lora's job was to set up parties in people's homes to sell the goods.

After a few weeks in the group, I popped off and told Lora that someday I was going to host a *Silpada* party for her. (Just for the record, never say that to someone like Lora, unless you really mean it.) A couple of weeks later following a meeting, Lora whipped out her calendar and said, "Okay! Let's plan your party!" I swallowed hard and agreed.

On my drive home that day, my brain went into creative overdrive. Lora's idea was that I could have some of my guy buddies come to the event to order jewelry for the ladies in their lives. But I wanted to also do something out of the ordinary. As if a jewelry party for guys wasn't enough!

Knowing that most guys like to eat—especially my friends—and some have adventuresome taste buds like I do, I came up with a plan. I called Lora and told her that I was going to bill the event as "Randy Mac's SPAM and Silpada Party." So that's the way it was promoted.

I went to the SPAM website (yes, there really is a SPAM web site) and found some *reeeeaaaaaaally* interesting recipes. I decided to make "SPAMaroni and Cheese Swaddlers," "SPAM Spuds," and "SPAMachos."

Once word got out about the party, some of the ladies started fussing because they were being barred from the get-together. Lora thought all the excitement was about her jewelry, but I'm pretty sure it was all about my cooking.

I eventually gave in and decided to let the women join us for the evening. And because I know that some of them wouldn't touch the main dishes—and because I'm such a gentleman—I decided to fix some treats that didn't contain SPAM. Of course, with me cooking, you might be safer going with what you *know* is in the dish before you opt for one you *aren't* sure exactly what's in it. (Hint: road kill.)

Again he asked, "What shall I compare the kingdom of God to? It is like yeast that a woman took and mixed into about sixty pounds of flour until it worked all through the dough." —Luke 13:20-21 NIV

As He often did, Jesus was using an analogy here to teach about God's Kingdom. But let's exchange the word "yeast" in verse 21 to connect to today's story and think about how the ladies wanted to come to the party in spite of the SPAM to see the jewelry.

"It is like SPAM that a man took and mixed into a pan of macaroni and cheese until it was worked throughout the entire dish."

If you like SPAM, you'd have no problem with this. But if you don't, you wouldn't touch any of it—no matter what other ingredients are used or how appetizing the dish looked.

Here's the connection and application: As an ambassador of Christ on this Earth, you are going to constantly encounter three groups of people.

1—Those who have no desire to come to "the party" (consider the Kingdom of God), because they are not interested in what you're offering (Jesus), no matter what food you're serving (a connection with you).

2—Those who will come to "the party," (consider the Kingdom of God) but they will not "eat" (accept Christ).

3—Those who decide to come to "the party," (consider the Kingdom of God) and do decide to "eat," (accept Christ) because they are at a place in their lives where they are ready for a relationship with God.

So, just keep inviting, serving, and loving the 1's and the 2's. Celebrate and savor when you get the privilege in taking part in new life with a 3. But until then, just know that for some people, it may look like you're serving up SPAM when they just want to keep looking pretty at the party.

Dear Jesus, help me to serve and love people through You. Strengthen me to never grow weary in inviting people into Your Kingdom. I want to see people come to know You, just like I did. Amen.

Week 6
Monday

The Grater Good

When Robbie and I were dating, her family lived a short distance from the church we attended. On weekends when she was home from college, I was usually invited to their house for lunch after church on Sundays. Robbie would help her mom get lunch ready, and I, of course, would hang around the kitchen. I was often given some helpful task, like putting ice in the tea glasses or getting the "brown-n-serve" rolls in the oven—and get them out before they burned. But on one particular Sunday, my mother-in-law-to-be put me in charge of making the cole slaw.

I took this as a sure sign that she was getting used to the idea of me being a part of the family. In hindsight, she really just needed someone to shred the cabbage. At any rate, I asked where the necessary equipment was for the job. I had seen my mom shred cabbage with a small, flat grater. "Mom," as I called Robbie's mother, so I could let her know that *I* was getting used to the idea of *her* being part of *my* family, handed me this gadget.

The hand crank turned a small barrel that had sides with grates. On the top was an opening where you placed the food item you were shredding. Hinged to the top was a small door with a handle on it. The idea was that you put the vegetable into the opening, using the little door to press them down against the sides of that barrel as you turned the crank. This action grates the veggies, while protecting your fingers. But there was a problem. Once you reached the halfway point, because the door was hinged on the top edge of the bin, you couldn't push straight down to grate. I surmised quickly that what I needed was leverage—

something that would allow me to push on the cabbage. So I grabbed a long spoon.

In what seemed like no time, I had all of the cabbage shredded and in the bowl. But at that moment, I realized the spoon—the *wooden* spoon—was considerably shorter than when I first took it from the drawer. Where did the wood go? As I surveyed the salad, little brown splinters were scattered throughout the cabbage. To salvage the slaw, we served it anyway. Everyone would take a bite, then work the splinters out to their lips, kind of like you do with seeds from a watermelon.

The next Sunday, Robbie's mom put me back on ice duty.

Jesus told a parable about a man's enemy coming into his field and planting weeds among his wheat. The problem was the weeds looked a lot like the wheat. When the servants discovered the problem and told the owner, he instructed them to just let it all grow, then to separate the weeds from the wheat during harvest. Later, the disciples asked Jesus what this parable meant. He answered…

"The one who sowed the good seed is the Son of Man. The field is the world, and the good seed stands for the people of the kingdom. The weeds are the people of the evil one, and the enemy who sows them is the devil. The harvest is the end of the age, and the harvesters are angels. "As the weeds are pulled up and burned in the fire, so it will be at the end of the age. The Son of Man will send out his angels, and they will weed out of his kingdom everything that causes sin and all who do evil. They will throw them into the blazing furnace, where there will be weeping and gnashing of teeth. Then the righteous will shine like the sun in the kingdom of their Father. Whoever has ears, let them hear." —Matthew 13:37-43 NIV

We spend a lot of time and energy sifting the good and evil in our own lives, others' lives, and the world. In today's passage, Jesus was stating that good and evil, the righteous and unrighteous, those for Jesus and those against Him, will live together, but in the end, he will sift them and throw out the weeds.

The more we learn to sift our own hearts through

the spirit of God, the better quality of life we can lead. Working the "splinters," or the "weeds" out of our own lives may be hard work at times, but always worth the effort as we walk with Jesus.

Heavenly Father, I know I need more of You and less of me. Help me to walk with You daily as we sift out the evil and put in the good that only You can give. Amen.

Week 6
Tuesday

Getting a-Head of Myself

Years ago while serving on a church staff in Haskell, Texas, I did a Sunday morning Gospel music show at the local radio station. I had a solid routine down every Sunday morning: I'd roll out of bed at 4:30 a.m., arrive at the station by 5:00, and get the coffee going (top priority). Then I'd turn the control room's ceiling fan on to medium speed (the high speed would blow the papers off the console) and gather up the music and commercials I'd be using that day.

One morning after I had gotten everything ready to go, I walked back into the control room to begin the show. I heard a small noise—the constant sound of clinking glass. I looked around the room; finally realizing it was coming from one of the tulip-shaped globes on the ceiling fan lights. With every revolution of the fan, the whole assembly would shake just enough to make the glass rattle. I looked on the floor and found a little screw that was obviously supposed to be securing that globe.

Standing on my tiptoes, I could reach the globe base, but after several seconds, I was still unable to get the screw started into the tiny threaded hole. With no hesitation, I pulled the chair from under the console desk, put it under the light, and stood up for a closer look, inserting my head right into that ceiling fan!

I learned that day a 5-blade fan running at medium speed can slap the back of one's head several times before the brain can signal to the victim to retreat. It's the same phenomenon that enacts the "3-second rule" we should use when following another vehicle, due to human reaction time.

I remember jumping down from that chair and grabbing my head, fully expecting to find blood. And I distinctly remember being thankful that the curtain in the control room window was still closed, so no one could see my Three Stooges routine. And it's a good thing I was on the radio and not a reality show! I can see the TV Guide now—"In this episode, Randy Mac sticks his head into a moving ceiling fan!"

Delilah had lulled Samson to sleep with his head resting in her lap. She signaled to one of the Philistine men as she began cutting off Samson's seven braids. And by the time she was finished, Samson's strength was gone. Delilah tied him up and shouted, "Samson, the Philistines are attacking! Samson woke up and thought, "I'll break loose and escape, just as I always do." He did not realize that the Lord had stopped helping him. —Judges 16:19-20 CEV

All I was trying to do was fix a ceiling fan when I stuck my head in it. And all Samson wanted to do was get a good night's sleep when he placed his head in Delilah's lap. There are many times in life when we get focused on one aspect of a situation, only to forget the one that can hurt us. We miss the big picture and forget our surroundings.

Today, is there anywhere you are so focused in a certain area that you're missing something that will really hurt you? God wants to warn us of impending danger, whether it's a bop on the head or a life-changing haircut. Stay close to Him today and mind what He says. That's always the safest place for any of us to be.

Dear God, help me to look for the big picture, yet keep me focused on the little things of life that can sneak up and hit me. I know that in You I can dwell in safety. Amen.

Week 6
Wednesday

Herbie's Ultimate Makeover

In 1979 B.C. (before children), Robbie and I lived in an apartment in Pasadena, Texas. One morning as I was leaving for work and walking down the hallway, I noticed a small card on a bulletin board. What caught my eye was the word "FREE" written in bold. I've always liked that word, so it got my attention. The card said someone in the complex was giving away a hamster *and* a cage. Whoa! What a deal! I wrote the number down, called the man, and assured him I'd come take advantage of his incredible offer as soon as I got home from work. He agreed to keep it for me. ... Yes!

Back at the apartments that afternoon, I went straight to get my new pet. I just *knew* Robbie would be excited. Or at least, I hoped. When the guy brought the cage to me, I was surprised to see an oily-looking critter inside. I asked, "Does he bite?" The man responded, "Oh, I don't know. I've never touched him." "Okay, well, thanks," I said and off we went.

I took the hamster home, but left it outside on the front porch—waiting to give him a big entrance. During supper, Robbie kept indicating that she could tell I wanted to tell her something. Truth was, I wasn't real sure I *did* want to tell her. But finally I got my nerve up and decided, rather than *tell* her, I'd just *show* her. I brought in Herbie, as I'd decided to call him, for the formal introduction. Robbie was underwhelmed. But she did approve me putting him in the extra bedroom, so I knew he was good for at least a one-night stay.

Early the next morning, while Rob was still sleeping, I decided Herb really needed to be cleaned. I took him into the guest bathroom, turned the warm water on in the basin, and grabbed a bottle of Revlon Flex shampoo. I stuck the little varmint under the stream of water and got him good and wet. Then I shot him with a bit of shampoo and began to rub him between my hands like a bar of soap. After "shampoo ... rinse ... repeat" (as per the instructions on the shampoo bottle), I knew Herbie was clean. But he had the appearance of the proverbial drowned rat. I knew I couldn't leave him wet. He might get sick. So I got out the big blow dryer.

Herbie kept trying to escape. He got out of my grip and ran up my arm at least four or five times before I got his new 'do dried. What was really cool is that the Revlon Flex had done quite a number on his hair. Now Herbie looked about three times as big as he did before his wash and set!

The next morning, as I was getting ready for work, I noticed I could see Herbie's cage in the reflection of the bathroom mirror. He was all cuddled up, sleeping in his warm bed of shredded paper. Well, that is until I fired up the blow dryer. When that whoosh of air came on, he jumped up and went into hamster panic mode. I don't think ol' Herb ever got over his makeover.

I prayed to the Lord, and he answered me. He freed me from all my fears. —Psalm 34:4 NLT

The word "fear" is used thousands of times in the Bible. Why? Because we all get scared a lot of a lot of things! We laugh at a hamster reacting in fear to a blow dryer, but we all have the same reactions to a lot of crazy things, because we connect it to an experience that frightens us.

We get the credit card bill and our pulse rate doubles.

We see that person's name come up on our ringing cell phone and we cringe.

The boss calls you into his office.

Your spouse says, "We need to talk."

The conversation with your child begins with, "Now, first, don't freak out..."

And of course, there are many serious and dreaded situations we anticipate coming.

We get trained to respond in fear just like that hairy hamster. Today, what is your biggest fear? What would trigger fright in your heart right now? Our verse tells us it's time to pray. Freedom from fear is found in faith. It won't always take away the situation, but it gives us a new way to respond.

Heavenly Father, there are so many things that can strike fear in my heart—some real, some not. Teach me to bring everything to you, so you can free me in faith from all my fears. Amen.

What You Can't See *Can* Hurt You

A few years back, I was a field trainer for a company that sets up pre-planned funerals for folks. I enjoyed the work and met a lot of great people over 10 years.

The company would bring in trainees to Cleburne, Texas, near where I lived. They would put them up in one particular hotel in the area. We would meet at 8:00 in the morning for a training session in the dining area. This would allow us to enjoy a light breakfast, and, of course, coffee, as we worked through the presentation of the program. Because of how often I was there, the hotel staff knew who I was.

One morning as I was about to start a new training session, I realized I had left something I needed in my truck. I excused myself from the class and began to walk very quickly through the lobby. While trying to retrieve my keys from my pocket and my mind thinking through where the item was that I needed, I was not paying close attention to where I was walking.

When I got to what I thought was the door, I just hit it with my forearm to knock it open. ... But it wasn't the door. It was the full-length window *beside* the door. ... And that window doesn't open.

A split-second after my arm hit the glass, my *head* hit the glass. The noise was very loud. The trainees came out of the dining area to see what had happened. The desk staff looked up in shock. There I stood, attempting to act cool, but failing. I checked for blood—all good. My pride was hurting badly, as was my forehead, where a lump was now growing. Fortunately, the glass didn't break. But there were two significantly large oily spots on the glass—one from my forehead and the other from my nose. (Just picture a large, oily "7".)

The young ladies who were in charge of cleaning the hotel spoke very little English. A few days later when I returned, I realized they had been cleaning *around* my face print, *intentionally* leaving my oily spot there on the glass.

One morning, one of those young ladies smiled at me, pointed at the spots, and said, "KA-BOOM!" I just smiled politely.

Talking with the lady at the front desk about me running into the window, she reassured me, "Well, don't feel bad. The other day we had a *dog* who did the same thing."

Yep. THAT made me feel better.

First pride, then the crash—the bigger the ego, the harder the fall. —Proverbs 16:18 MSG

The Randy Mac version might read: "First pride, then KA-BOOM—the bigger they are, the larger the oily spot."

While I really wasn't struggling with pride that day, it is still a good example of how we can walk through life not paying attention to the things we should be. And isn't self-centered to just go through the motions, not focusing on what we should?

When we run into windows, call someone by the wrong name, or get to the checkout and realize our wallet is in the car, we are humbled. Lots of every day incidents keep our pride in check.

Have you been humbled lately? Is there an "oily spot" somewhere from your pride running into something or someone? Did someone laugh and say, "KA-BOOM" to you recently?

It's important we constantly check ourselves for the big ole "I" in the middle of pride; places where we focus on what we want and not what others need; situations where God's will should be placed first, not our own. When you realize you have an "oily spot," just ask God to forgive you, get your priorities back in line, and walk on ... through the door!

Lord Jesus, remind me when the "I" in pride starts showing up that a crash won't be far behind. Teach me to stay humble and lean on Your wisdom and grace. I want to walk with You, so I won't fall for anything. Amen.

Week 6
Friday

Ironing Out Our Issues

I'm not sure how it happens. Obviously, my brain doesn't function like everyone else's. Not only does this add to my adventures in life, but it also gives me stories to share with my audiences when I perform. Some of them, though, sound so ridiculous that some people question their validity ... and my sanity. I'll even hold my right hand in the air to swear I'm telling the truth, so help me, God. So on this one, just picture me standing with my right hand in the air!

Years ago, I was a regular guest every summer at the Baptist Family Camp at Paisano in west Texas, between Alpine and Marfa. This is a large camp with as many as 1500 campers on site for the week. They would bring me in to lead out in the youth ministry events. These took place in the morning with afternoons and evenings designated as free time. At night those who wanted, would head over to the open-air tabernacle for the worship service. One evening Robbie and I decided that we would go to the evening service.

I fired up the iron to touch up my blue jeans. After I put on my jeans and boots, I grabbed one of my "polo" golf shirts. After I pulled it on, I realized there was a substantial wrinkle running across the right side of the chest area. At that moment my brain convinced me that I could probably iron it—while I wore it. After all, why waste the time and energy to actually take the shirt off?

I knew the iron was hot, because I had *just* ironed my jeans. Grabbing the iron, I took a deep breath, stuck out my chest as far as I could, and ran it over the wrinkle. I exhaled after each pass and then I'd take a big breath for the next one. The wrinkle *was* getting smaller, but wouldn't completely go away. Then my brain suggested that perhaps I should put some water on it. I walked into the little bathroom in our cabin, got some water in my hand, and applied it to the area.

I walked back out and grabbed the iron again. It was at that moment I learned if you put a hot iron to something

78

wet you are wearing, the intense heat will cook your flesh underneath— immediately and thoroughly. I closed my eyes, gritted my teeth, and held my chest, as the intense pain grew.

When it finally began to ease up, I was able to slowly open my now tear-filled eyes. As my vision returned, I realized my wife had been watching the entire time and had seen the whole thing. She sat there on the edge of the bed, shaking her head, saying nothing. She didn't need to. Lesson learned—once again—the hard way.

Sometimes it takes a painful experience to make us change our ways. —Proverbs 20:30 GNT

Isn't it ironic that we don't—or won't—work hard to repent of sin and change our hearts when life is going great? Nothing makes us question our choices like pain, hurt, crisis, or failure.

God sees an area we desperately need to change, because it is not good for us, or those around us, so He starts to speak to us and work in us. But we miss it or dismiss it. Then we pick up the iron, so to speak, in a weak moment and, once again, we get burned. The bad thing is, too often, our decision hurts others too. I would imagine, when Robbie saw me wince in pain from that iron, she cringed a little too.

Is there anywhere in your life where God might be trying to help you learn a lesson the easy way? Anywhere He might be asking you to change something and you aren't paying attention? Take it from me—it's a smart move to try and make the right decision *before* the pain starts!

Heavenly Father, thank You that You want the best for me always. Thank You that I can trust You are trying to help me and never want to hurt me. Forgive me when I ignore Your warnings and turn my back on You. That choice hurts You, hurts me, and others. Give me eyes to see You and ears to hear You, to change before the pain starts. Amen.

Week 6
The Weekend

My Mama's Mouth of Mirth

I was with my mom when she died. I held her hand in the nursing home in Glen Rose, Texas and watched her slip from here to Heaven. I have so many great memories of her.

As a small kid, I wore overalls a lot. Growing up down in the Gulf Coast area around Pasadena, Texas, rain was a common event. When the heavy downpours would run off our yard, it wouldn't be long before the crawfish would show up. On occasion, we'd find babies with their mama. One day, I caught one. There's something about five-year-old boys that makes them think anything living can become a pet. I needed a place to keep my new critter, while my brothers and I went looking for more. The next day, when Mom took the clean clothes out of our dryer, she informed me the bib of my overalls was not a good home for a baby crawfish.

Then there was "Aroma," my pet skunk. (Remember my locker at school?)

And the spreading adder snake that got loose in our house for a few days.

And the time I drove Mama's car through the living room wall.

I created a lot of adventure for my mom. But, fortunately for us all, she had a great sense of humor, along with a quick wit. I think it was her survival mechanism. She was seldom speechless and rarely held back what she thought.

Many who knew her remember the random sayings she'd throw out. Some were borrowed, but others were definitely original. One night at the supper table my brother, Charles, was being a bit "lippy." Mom told him, "Alright, son, you're gonna fool around and flub your dub and when you do, it's gonna be YOUR dub that you're gonna flub." We all just sat there in stunned silence. Charles included. He quieted down, not wanting anything to do with flubs or dubs.

Some of her most memorable quips of agreement include, "whatever melts your butter" and "whatever floats your boat." During her last few weeks of life, she would occasionally have to spend a day or two in the hospital. Although she was usually in good spirits, she was also often confused. One day as a nurse was leaving Mom's room, she explained some procedures they'd be going through a little later. With a very pleasant, up-beat voice Mom said, "Whatever melts your boat." That moment still makes me smile.

Of all the lessons I've learned in this life, one of the most important is building great memories with, and for, those we live with and love. Of all the things in my life I'm thankful for, one is the fact that my mom always did just that. I can't wait to see her again one day in Heaven, but for now, her memories make me laugh, flub my dub, and melt my boat!

A cheerful heart is good medicine... —Proverbs 17:22a
NIV

Who doesn't like to be around someone with a cheerful heart, right? Laughter and humor are medicine for our souls where the prescription is really easy to get filled!

Think for a moment about the people in your life who make you laugh; those who make you forget about your troubles for a few minutes by saying something quirky or comical. Do you need a little more laughter in your life these days? The best way for this to happen is to find more ways to laugh—or even laugh at yourself. I know I sure enjoy doing that. So did mama.

Father, you call us Your friends, so that means You can laugh with us. Help me today to light up every place I go with Your good medicine. Help me to bring more laughter into the lives of those around me and not take myself so seriously. Amen.

We hope and pray you have enjoyed the *Livin' It Up!* devotional book. We want to encourage you to keep spending daily time in God's Word and in prayer, getting closer to Jesus. If you read the Gospel presentation in this book (next page) and prayed to receive Christ, please let someone know—a Christian friend, a local pastor, or priest.

Then tell your family and friends about your decision to follow Christ. Let me know about your decision, any comments regarding this book, or come see us at an event sometime. Visit Randymac.com. And always remember—keep *Livin' It Up!*

How to Have a Relationship with Jesus Christ

I believe that, probably, the most memorized verse in all the bible is *John 3:16*. *"For God so loved the world that he gave his only begotten Son, that whosoever believes in Him shall not perish, but have eternal life." NAS*

Jesus was speaking to a very religious man named Nicodemus—a great, well-known teacher of Jewish law. This verse is a very powerful statement that speaks of God's incredibly great love for ALL mankind.

Earlier in that same chapter, Nicodemus had approached Jesus privately about this "new kingdom" He'd been talking about, where everything is perfect—and lasts forever. Nicodemus was wondering how *he* could be part of such a kingdom.

Jesus' response? *"Truly, truly, I say to you, unless one is born again he cannot see the kingdom of God." John 3:3 NAS*

Not be a good man.

Not be a good church member.

Not give your money away.

Not be kind to others.

Not be baptized, sprinkled, dipped, or otherwise.

Jesus said that for Nicodemus—or anyone else—to have a home in Heaven, they would HAVE to be born again. Period.

So what does that mean?

Being born again happens when a person receives a brand new life in Jesus Christ. *That* happens when anyone realizes they have unforgiven sin in their life (Romans 3:23), and that there's a great price to pay for sin (Romans 6:23). There IS a way to have sin removed, but man CANNOT do it himself (Ephesians 2:8-9). Man HAS to have a Savior. Thus JESUS.

"For whoEVER will call upon the Name of the Lord WILL BE SAVED!" (Romans 10:13) (Emphasis mine.)

God wants to have a personal relationship with YOU. He wants YOU to be born again—to have a reservation in Heaven for eternity. If you've never—by your own choosing—entered into a personal relationship with God through Jesus Christ, maybe right now you feel that nudging in your spirit to call on Jesus, asking Him to be your Savior. If so, just say something like this to Him ...

Lord Jesus, Please forgive me of my sins and save me from eternal separation from God. I now know You died on the cross for my sins and I thank You for that. I want to know You as MY personal Savior and I want to know God through You. I give you my life—completely. I choose to follow You for the rest of my days. Thank You for loving me and forgiving me. Thank You for a brand new start! Teach me Your ways and help me to always follow You. In Jesus Name. AMEN.

If you just committed your life to Christ and received His cleansing and forgiveness, then congratulations! We'd love to know about your decision, so we can share in your joy. Please send us a note to randymac@randymac.com. God Bless!!!

Made in the USA
San Bernardino, CA
12 September 2015